PARENTING
WITH
LOVE AND LOGIC

PARENTING WITH LOVE AND LOGIC

Teaching Children Responsibility

Foster W. Cline, M.D. and Jim Fay

P.O. Box 35007, Colorado Springs, CO 80935

OUR GUARANTEE TO YOU

We believe so strongly in the message of our books that we are making this quality guarantee to you. If for any reason you are disappointed with the content of this book, return the title page to us with your name and address and we will refund to you the list price of the book. To help us serve you better, please briefly describe why you were disappointed. Mail your refund request to: PiñonPress, P.O. Box 35002, Colorado Springs, CO 80935.

Library of Congress Catalog Card Number:
    92-60546
ISBN 08910-93117

Cover Photograph: © Tony Stone Worldwide,
Jo Browne / Mick Smee

The actual text of *Parenting with Love and Logic* was written by Tom
Raabe.

Scripture in this publication is from the *New Revised Standard Version*,
copyright 1989 by the Division of Christian Education of the National
Council of the Churches of Christ in the USA, used by permission, all
rights reserved.

Cline, Foster.
    Parenting with love and logic : teaching
    children responsibility / by Foster Cline
    and Jim Fay.
        229 p. ; ill. ; 24 cm.
        Includes index.
        ISBN 0-89109-311-7 :
        1. Parent and child. 2. Parenting.   I. Fay, Jim.   II. Title.
    HQ755.85.C58   1990
    n-us-co   90-61765
                                                            CIP

Printed in the United States of America

22 23 24 25 / 06 05 04 03 02

CONTENTS

Love-and-Logic Tips

AUTHORS

Foster W. Cline, M.D., is an internationally recognized child and adult psychiatrist. He is a consultant to mental health organizations, parents' groups, and schools across North America. He specializes in working with difficult children.

Jim Fay has thirty-one years of experience as an educator and principal. He is recognized as one of America's top educational consultants and has won many awards in the education field.

To my wife, Shirley,
whose love, support, and wisdom
have always been a source
of motivation and strength.
— Jim Fay

To all the parents
and children
who were my teachers
and to my wife
who gave support.
— Foster W. Cline

INTRODUCTION

Ours may be the first generation of parents who cannot even ponder parenting the way our parents did and be successful at it. For hundreds of years, rookie parents learned the fine points of child-rearing by example; they took the techniques their parents had used on them and applied them to their children.

Today, this approach is more apt to bomb than to boom. Many of us, when we meet failure, throw up our hands in frustration and say, "I can't understand it. It worked for my dad!"

Yes, it did. But things have changed. The human rights revolution, the communication explosion, changes in the family — these, and many other factors, have radically changed how our children view life. Kids are forced to grow up quicker these days, so they need to learn sooner how to cope with the tremendous challenges and pressures of contemporary life. The impact of divorce and other changes in the family have been dramatic.

Effective parents must learn to use different techniques with kids who live in today's complex, rapidly changing world.

That's where *parenting with love and logic* comes in. Why the terms *love* and *logic*? Effective parenting centers around love: love that is not permissive, love that doesn't tolerate disrespect, but also love that is powerful enough to allow kids to make mistakes and permit them to live with the consequences of those mistakes. The logic is centered in the consequences themselves. Most mistakes do have logical consequences. And those consequences, when accompanied by empathy — our compassionate understanding of the child's disappointment, frustration, and pain — hit home with mind-changing power. It's never too late to begin parenting with love and logic.

This book is written in two parts. In the first, we will lay out our concepts on parenting in general terms, centering on building self-concept, separation of problems, use of thinking words, offering choices, and meeting the consequences of our kids' mistakes with empathy. These are the building blocks of effective parenting. Part one also contains extra tidbits of information, "Love-and-Logic Tips," which add flesh to the bone of many love-and-logic principles.

In the second part, we get practical. The forty-one love-and-logic pearls offer everyday strategies for dealing with problems most parents will face during the first twelve or so years of their children's lives. These pearls build on the general ideas developed in the first half of the book and should be used only after the first part has been read and understood.

Parenting with love and logic is not a foolproof system

that works every time. In fact, it is not a comprehensive system at all. Our approach is more of an attitude that, when carried out in the context of a healthy, loving relationship with our children, will allow them to grow in maturity as they grow in years. It will teach them to think, to decide, and to live with their decisions. In short, it will teach them responsibility, and that's what parenting is all about. If we can teach our kids responsibility, we've accomplished a great share of our parental task.

The Bible provides insight on many parenting issues. Much of what this book teaches is summarized beautifully in a familiar Old Testament proverb:

Train children in the right way
and when old, they will not stray.
(Proverbs 22:6)

What greater gift could parents give their children than the opportunity for a joyful, productive, and responsible adult life? We believe the principles of *Parenting with Love and Logic* will help achieve that result.

PART I

❖

The Love-and-Logic Parent

1

Parenting:
Joy or Nightmare?

❖

A wise child loves discipline,
but a scoffer does not listen to rebuke.
PROVERBS 13:1

It's Saturday at the local supermarket. Two boys, ages five and seven, have declared war. Like guerrillas on a raiding party, they sneak from aisle to aisle, hiding behind displays and squeaking their tennies on the tile floor. A crash — the result of a game of "shopping cart chicken" — punctures the otherwise calming background Muzak.

The mother, having lost sight of this self-appointed commando unit, abandons her half-filled cart. As she rounds a corner, her scream turns the heads of other shoppers: "Don't get lost! Don't touch that! *You* — get over here!"

The mom races for the boys, and as she's about to grab two sweaty necks, they turn to Tactic B — "the split up," a 1990s version of "divide and conquer." Now she must run in two directions to shout at them. Wheezing with exertion, she corrals the younger one, who just blitzed the cereal section, leaving a trail of boxes. But when she returns him to her cart, the older boy is gone. She locates him in produce, rolling seedless grapes like marbles across the floor.

After scooping up Boy Number Two and carrying him back, you guessed it, Boy Number One has disappeared. Mom sprints from her cart once more. Finally, after threatening murder and the pawning of their Nintendo game, the boys are gathered.

The battle's not over. Tactic C follows — the "fill the cart when Mom's not looking" game. Soon M & M's, Oreos, vanilla wafers, and jumbo Snickers bars are piled high. Mom races back and forth reshelving the treats. Then come boyish smirks and another round of threats from Mom: "Don't do that! I'm going to slap your hands!" And in a death cry of desperation, "You're never going to leave the house again for the rest of your lives!"

Frazzled, harried, and broken, Mom finally surrenders and buys off her precious flesh and blood with candy bars — a cease fire that guarantees enough peace to finish her rounds.

ARE WE HAVING FUN YET?

Ah, yes, parenting — the joys, the rewards. We become parents with optimism oozing from every pore. During late night feedings and sickening diaper changes, we know we are laying the groundwork for a lifelong relationship that will bless us when our hair disappears or turns gray. We look forward to times of tenderness and times of love. To shared joys and shared disappointments. To hugs and encouragement, words of comfort and soul-filled conversations. When the flesh-of-our-flesh looks into our eyes, we want the love that passes between us to be almost palpable.

But the joys of parenting were far from the mind of

this grocery store mom. No freshly scrubbed cherubs flitted through her life, hanging on every soft word dropping from "mommy's" lips. Where was that gratifying, loving, personal relationship between parent and child? The sublime joys of parenting were obliterated by a more immediate concern: survival.

This was parenting—the nightmare.

Scenes like this happen to the best of us. When they do, we may want to throw our hands in the air and scream, "Kids! Are they worth the pain?"

Sometimes kids can be a bigger hassle than a house with one shower. When we think of the enormous love we pump into our children's lives and then receive in return too much sassy, disobedient, unappreciative behavior, we can get pretty burned out on the whole process. Besides riddling our lives with day-to-day hassles, kids present us with perhaps *the* big-time challenge of our adulthood: *How do we raise our children to be responsible adults?*

Through the miracle of birth, we are given a tiny, defenseless babe, a stranger in an alien world, totally dependent on us for every physical need. We have a mere eighteen years *at most* to ready that suckling for a world that can be cruel and heartless. That child's success in the real world hinges in large part on the job we do as parents. Raising responsible, well-rounded kids sends a sobering shiver of responsibility right up the old parental spine. How many of us have felt nauseous after this devilish thought: *If I can't handle a five-year-old in a grocery store, what am I going to do with a fifteen-year-old who seems to have an enormous understanding of sex and is counting the days until he gets a driver's license?*

PUTTING THE FUN BACK INTO PARENTING

All is not so bleak. Trust us! There's hope, shining beacon bright, at the end of the tunnel of parental frustration. Parenting doesn't have to be drudgery. Children *can* grow to be thinking, responsible adults. We can help them do it without living through an eighteen-year horror movie.

Parenting with love and logic is all about raising responsible kids. It's a win-win philosophy. Parents win because they love in a healthy way and establish effective control over their kids, without resorting to the anger and threats that will haunt them later through rebellious teenage behavior. Kids win because at an early age they learn responsibility and the logic of life by solving their own problems. Thus they acquire the tools for coping with the real world.

Parents and kids can establish a rewarding relationship built on love and trust in the process. What a deal! Parenting with love and logic puts the fun back in parenting.

2

MISSION POSSIBLE: RAISING RESPONSIBLE KIDS

❖

Train children in the right way,
and when old, they will not stray.
PROVERBS 22:6

A ll loving parents face essentially the same challenge: How do we raise children who have their heads on straight and will have a good chance to make it in the big world? Every sincere mom and dad strives to attain this goal. We must equip our darling offspring to make the move from total dependence on us to independence—from being controlled to controlling themselves.

Let's face it, in this incredibly complex, fast-changing age, responsible kids are the only ones who will be able to handle the real world that awaits them. Life-and-death decisions confront teenagers—and even younger children—at every turn. Drugs, premarital sex, riding in fast cars, alcohol—many of the pressures and temptations of adult life are thrown at kids every day. The statistics on teen suicide bear out the deadly seriousness of the parental task. How will our children handle such intense pressures? What choices will they make when faced with these life-and-death decisions? What will they do when we are no longer pouring wise words into their ears? Will merely telling them to be responsible get the job done? These are the questions that should guide the development of our parenting philosophy.

I (Jim) was struck by the gravity of the parenting task recently when my teenage son asked to use the family car to go to a party. "It's the party of the year," Charlie said. "Everybody who's anybody will be there."

I trust Charlie and would have loaned him the car, but I had a speaking engagement and couldn't oblige. Charlie's mother, Shirley, had plans of her own for the second car.

"Why don't you hitch a ride with Randy," I suggested, referring to Charlie's best friend.

Charlie shook his head. "That's okay. I understand. I guess I won't go," he said and went to his room. I knew something was up. This was *the* party of the year, so I talked to Charlie and pried loose some more information. Randy, it seems, had been drinking at parties, and Charlie decided he'd rather stay home than risk the danger of riding with a friend who drank and drove.

The night of that party, Randy, plied with booze, drove himself and five passengers off the side of a mountain at eighty miles per hour.

Unfortunately, many kids arrive at their challenging and life-threatening teenage years with no clue as to how to make decisions. They "know better" but still try drugs. They ignore good advice from parents and other adults and dabble with sex. Why do young people sometimes seem so stupidly self-destructive? The tragic truth is that many of these foolish choices are the first real decisions they have ever made. In childhood, decisions were always made for them—by well-meaning parents like us. We must understand that making good choices is like any other activity:

It has to be learned. The teenagers who make the wrong choice on alcohol are probably the same children who never learned how to keep their hands out of the cookie jar.

Parents who take their parenting job seriously want to raise responsible kids, kids who at any age can confront the important decisions of their lives with maturity and good sense.

WE HAVE MET THE ENEMY

Good parents learn to do what is best for their children. Those little tykes, so innocent and playful at our feet, will someday grow up. We want to do everything humanly possible for our children, so that someday they can strut confidently into the real world. And we do it all in the name of love. But love can get us into trouble—not love per se, but *how we show it*. Our noble intentions are often our own worst enemy when it comes to raising responsible kids.

Contrary to popular opinion, many of the worst kids—the most disrespectful and rebellious—often come from homes where they are shown love, sometimes unbounded love. It's just the wrong kind of love. How can this happen?

INEFFECTIVE PARENTING STYLES

Helicopter Parents
Some parents think *love* means rotating their lives around their children. They are helicopter parents. They hover over and rescue their children whenever trouble arises. They're forever running lunches and permission slips and home-work assignments to school; they're always pulling their children out of jams; not a day goes by when they're not protecting little junior from something—usually from a learning experience the child needs or deserves. As soon as their children send up an SOS flare, helicopter parents, who are hovering nearby, swoop in and shield the children

from teachers, playmates, and other elements that appear hostile.

While today these "loving" parents may feel they are easing their children's path into adulthood, tomorrow the same children will be leaving home and wasting the first eighteen months of their adult life, flunking out of college or meandering about "getting their heads together." Such children are unequipped for the challenges of life. Their learning opportunities were stolen from them in the name of love.

The irony is that helicopter parents are often viewed by others as model parents. They feel uncomfortable imposing consequences. When they see their children hurting, they hurt too. So they bail them out.

But the real world does not run on the bail-out principle. Traffic tickets, overdue bills, irresponsible people, crippling diseases, taxes—these and other normal events of adult life usually do not disappear because a loving benefactor bails us out. Helicopter parents fail to prepare their kids to meet that kind of world.

Drill Sergeant Parents

Other parents are like drill sergeants. These, too, love their children. They feel that the more they bark and the more they control, the better their kids will be in the long run. "These kids will be disciplined," the drill sergeant says. "They'll know how to act right." Indeed, they are constantly *told* what to do.

When drill sergeant parents talk to children, their words are often filled with putdowns and I-told-you-so's. These parents are into power! If children don't do what they're told, drill sergeant parents are going to—doggone it all—make them do it.

Kids of drill sergeant parents, when given the chance to think for themselves, often make horrendous decisions—to the complete consternation and disappointment of their parents. But it makes sense. These kids are rookies in the world of decisions. They've never had to think—the drill sergeant took care of that. The kids have been ordered around all of their lives. They're as dependent on their parents when they enter the real world as the kids of helicopter parents.

Both of these types of parents send messages to their children—all in the name of love—about what they think their kids are capable of. The message the helicopter parent sends to the child is, "You are fragile and can't make it without me." The drill sergeant's message is, "You can't think for yourself, so I'll do it for you."

While both of these parental types may successfully control the children in the early years, they have thrown major obstacles into the kids' path once they hit the "Puberty Trail." Helicopter children become adolescents unable to cope with outside forces, unable to think for themselves or handle their own problems. Drill sergeant kids, who did a lot of saluting when they were young, will do a lot of saluting when teenagers. But the salute is different—a raised fist or a crude gesture involving the middle finger.

THE PARADOX OF SUCCESS AND FAILURE

Although we're tempted to do otherwise, it's time for us (Foster and Jim) to admit that there is no surefire, absolute, guaranteed-or-your-money-back approach to raising responsible children. No expert—least of all us—in the field can honestly say, "If you operate this way, it'll work every time." Just because we do something correctly doesn't mean it will work out the way we'd hoped.

We all have examples of parents, employing very faulty parenting techniques, whose children come out smelling like roses. Others, who do everything "right," raise kids that would make Attila the Hun look like an eagle scout.

Nothing in parenting is sure. However, we raise the odds in parenting responsible kids when we take thoughtful risks. We do that when we allow our children—get this—to fail. In fact, *unless we allow them to fail, sometimes grandiosely fail, we cannot allow our children to choose success.*

LOVE-AND-LOGIC TIP 1
Unfortunately, When Our Gut Talks, Our Head Listens
The techniques of parenting with love and logic may rub some parents the wrong way. Allowing kids to fail with love, letting the SLOs (significant learning opportunities) do the teaching, treating themselves right as a way of modeling healthy adult behavior—these principles can go against the parental grain.

Most of us raise our children based on our gut reactions. But how do we know whether such responses are trustworthy or just the result of bad lasagna? Actually, adult "gut reactions" are the result of childhood responses to family emotions and interactions. Therefore, "gut feel" is more valid if we had a happy childhood and presently have peaceful and rewarding relationships at home and elsewhere. Sure we all will "nerd out" more often with children if our own childhood and/or present home life are in turmoil, but generally our actions with our kids will be fine.

If, on the other hand, we react to our childhood by saying, "I sure want to do things differently with my kid than my mom and dad did with me," then our gut reactions will probably be untrustworthy and faulty. Those instinctive reactions come from our parents—and we hated the way they parented us!

Don't be alarmed if you feel uneasy with some of the techniques in this book for parenting with love and logic. In fact, if you want to raise your kids in ways different from the way you were raised, your uneasiness probably confirms that you're on the right track.

God gave all humans—His supreme creation—considerable freedom, and that includes the opportunity to goof up. Failure and success are two sides of the same coin. If there had been no forbidden tree in the Garden of Eden, humanity would have had no opportunity to make responsible or irresponsible choices. When Adam and Eve made the wrong choice, God allowed them to suffer the consequences. Although He did not approve of their disobedience, He loved them enough to let them make a decision and to live with the results.

God's love in the garden sets the example for all parents to follow: He allowed Adam and Eve the freedom to make the choice. In a similar way, if we give children freedom and loving acceptance, they will make choices and do things we will not approve of.

As our children grow older and gain more power over their lives and environment, the correct exercise of their ability to make decisions becomes even more important for them. Just as God gave us a good mind and the ability to excel, He has given us the right, or at least the capability, to blow up the planet. However, a race capable of blowing up the planet is also capable of flying to Saturn. High success and high achievement carry with them the risks of abysmal losses.

On a different scale, the issue of the "forbidden fruit" may be drugs, a particular friend, or any number of other choices kids face. Parents who seek to ensure the success of their children narrow their choices by half. For their children to make their own decisions, they will have to exert independence by choosing, consciously, to fail!

I (Jim) used to insist that my son Charlie dress for the weather on chilly Colorado mornings. "Charlie," I'd say, "it's cold out this morning. You'd better wear your heavy coat." Sure enough, he'd grab his little slicker—the lightest coat he owned—and waltz out the door.

Unwittingly, I was taking away his best choice. I thought I was ensuring that he would be warm waiting for the bus, but he chose to be cold instead. He was exerting his free will.

But I wised up. When I said, "Charlie, it's twenty degrees out. You might want to wear a coat," this offered him a range of choices from worst to best (kids always seem to discount the first option we give them), he decided to exert his will with a warm coat.

So, the paradox is that *parents who try to ensure their children's successes, often raise unsuccessful kids!* But the loving and *concerned* parents who allow for failure wind up with kids who tend to choose success. These are the parents who take thoughtful risks. As God gives each of us choices, we can do no less for our own loved children.

The parenting with love and logic approach helps kids raise their odds of becoming thinking individuals who choose success. As parents, this means we must allow for failures and help our kids make the most of them during their elementary school days, when the price tags are still reasonable.

LEARNING AT AFFORDABLE PRICES

Today's kids suffer from inflation. The cost of learning how to live in our world is going up daily. The price a child pays today to learn about friendships, school, learning, commitment, decision making, and responsibility is the cheapest it will ever be. Tomorrow it's always higher.

The older a child gets, the bigger the decisions become, and the graver the consequences of those decisions. Little children can make many mistakes at affordable prices. They can pick themselves up and try again if things don't work out. Usually all they're out is some temporary pain and a few tears. This is easy to illustrate.

A smart-mouthed boy of five who wises off to bigger, older neighborhood boys will, if left to handle his own problem, learn a major-league lesson in respect. Bigger boys rub their hands with glee at the prospect of teaching smart-aleck kids lessons. The lesson may cost—a bloody nose or a black eye for the smaller child—but the price is affordable.

That price is too high for some parents. They protect. They reason, "I love him. I don't want little Johnny to learn the hard way." They yell at the neighborhood boys, "You kids be nice to Johnny. If you can't be nice, I'm going to tell your parents." As a result, the smart-aleck kid loses the opportunity to learn a lesson at blue-light-special prices.

Now he may have to learn it at age fifteen, and anyone who has seen fifteen-year-old boys go at it knows that the price tag will be far more expensive.

True, it's painful to watch our kids learn through natural consequences or, as we call them, significant learning opportunities (SLOs). But that pain is part of the price we must pay to raise responsible kids.

We have a choice, though. We can hurt a little as we watch them learn life's lessons now. Or we can hurt a lot as we watch them grow up as individuals who are unable to care for themselves.

LOVE-AND-LOGIC TIP 2
You Can Pay Me Now, or You Can Pay Me Later
Sylvia has eight kids. Every time I (Jim) visit her house, I see her handing out money to the kids. One day I asked, "What is this with you dishing out money all the time?"

"We give our kids loans in the household because they're learning about the world of finance," Sylvia answered while handing fifty cents to a small boy. "Our loans are just like those at the First National Bank, with due dates, promissory notes, and collateral. Why, the other day I repossessed a twenty-nine-dollar tape recorder."

"Must have been sad for the kid," I said.

"Not really," Sylvia replied. "That's a gift to him because now my son, who's only ten years old, knows all about the responsibility of paying back his loans. He knows all about promissory notes and collateral, and even repossession—and it only cost him a twenty-nine-dollar tape recorder.

"The neighbor kid," Sylvia continued, "learned the same lesson when the bank came and repossessed his $4,900 Camaro. He's twenty-six, but his parents protected him when he was young. My son has a sixteen-year head start on the guy."

TO PROTECT THEM IS NOT TO LOVE THEM

Many parents confuse *love, protection,* and *caring.* These concepts are not synonymous. Parents may refuse to allow their children to fail because they see such a response as uncaring.

Thus they overcompensate with worry and hyper-concern. What these parents are doing, in reality, is meeting their own selfish needs. They make more work for themselves and will, in the long run, raise children who make their own lives more work. Protection is not synonymous with caring, but both are a part of love.

Let's look at the way God operates. If we ask ourselves, "Does God care about us?" we'd probably respond, "Sure, God cares a lot about us." But if we then ask ourselves, "Would He let us jump off a cliff tonight?" we'd all have to admit, "Yeah, now that you mention it, He probably would." So does He *care*? Of course He does! Yet God loves without being overly protective.

Caring for our children does not equate to protecting them from every possible misstep that they could make in growing up. At birth, of course, responsible parents must respond to their infant with total protectiveness. Every problem the *infant* encounters really *is* the parents' problem. If parents do not protect the infant, the infant will die.

However, as children grow—beginning at about nine months of age with very simple choices—the parents must make a gentle, gradual transition to allowing their children the privilege of solving their own problems. By the time children are eleven or twelve years old, they should be able to make most decisions without parental input. Actually, to be truthful, parental love and attitude determine how almost all children will handle almost all problems through early adolescence.

For instance, I (Foster) have watched young mothers handling their toddlers as they wobble onto the ice on their first skates. These moms can be classified in two groups: the "Kaboomers!" and the "Are you hurts?"

Once the toddlers make their inevitable crash on the ice, one group of young moms, worried to death at the side of the rink, yells, "Are you hurt?" And the toddlers, scrunching up their faces and sliding back toward Mom, say, in that distinctive toddler way, "Yeah, come to think of it, I *am* hurt."

The other group of moms merely shouts "Kaboom!" when the children go down, and their youngsters pick themselves up, dust a few flakes off the old bottom, and go on skating—often saying, "Yeah, kaboom!" in agreement.

The first group of children learned that a fall is a painful experience. The second group learned from their mistakes, not concentrating on the pain and parental rescue. The problem is, rescuing parents often rescue out of their own needs. They like "healing hurts." They are parents who *need to be needed*, not parents who *want to be wanted*.

When young people reach high school, if love has been shown primarily by protection, they may be irreparably damaged. Parents of junior high or high school children who must concern themselves with issues like clothing, television habits, homework, teeth brushing, haircuts, and the like have "at risk" children on their hands. At the very least, these children are not going to be much fun for their future spouse.

The challenge of parenting is to love kids enough to allow them to fail. To stand back, however painful it may be, and let SLOs (significant learning opportunities) build our children.

RESPONSIBILITY CANNOT BE TAUGHT

Parents are forever moaning about their children's inability to absorb parental words of wisdom. It seems we can tell daughter Cindy a hundred times not to forget something, and sure enough, she walks out the door without it. We tell son Mike to show some respect, and he answers, "Why do I have to do that? You're living in the Dark Ages!"

One thing for sure we can't tell kids is "be responsible." It doesn't work. Have you ever noticed that the parents who yell the loudest about responsibility seem to have the most irresponsible kids? The most responsible children usually come from families where parents almost never use the word *responsibility*.

It's a fact: *Responsibility cannot be taught; it must be caught.*

Although it's hard to figure out at times, the hardest things in the world to learn are the things we are told we must do. To help a child gain responsibility we must offer that child opportunities to be responsible.

That's the key. Parents who raise responsible kids spend very little time and energy worrying about their kids' responsibilities. They worry more about how to let the children encounter SLOs for their *irresponsibility*. They are involved with their kids, certainly, lovingly using good judgment as to when their children are ready to learn the next level of life's lessons. But they don't spend their time reminding them or worrying for them. In a subtle way they're saying, "I'm sure you'll remember on your own, but if you don't you'll surely learn something from the experience." These parents help their children understand that they can solve their own problems. These parents are sympathetic, but they don't solve their kids' problems.

Children who grow in responsibility also grow in self-esteem—a prerequisite for achievement in the real world. As self-esteem and self-confidence grow, children are better able to make it once the parental ties are cut.

3

RESPONSIBLE CHILDREN
FEEL GOOD
ABOUT THEMSELVES

❖

Even children make themselves known
by their acts,
by whether what they do
is pure and right.
PROVERBS 20:11

There are two types of kids in this world. One type gets up in the morning, looks in the mirror, and says, "Hey, look at that dude. He's all right! I like that guy, and I bet other people will like him too."

The other type, when she looks in the mirror, says, "Oh no, look at that girl. I really don't like what I see, and I bet other people won't like her either."

Two radically different outlooks on life; two radically different self-concepts. Children with a poor self-concept often forget to do homework, bully other kids, argue with teachers and parents, steal, and withdraw into themselves whenever things get rocky—irresponsible kids in all they do. Children with a good self-concept tend to have a lot of friends, do their chores regularly, and don't get into trouble in school—they take responsibility as a matter of course in their daily lives.

Although this may seem simplistic, there is a direct correlation between self-concept and performance in school, at home, on the playground, or wherever children may be. Kids learn best and are responsible when they feel good about themselves.

When parenting with love and logic, we strive to offer our children a chance to develop that needed positive self-concept. With love enough to allow the children to fail, with love enough to allow the consequences of their actions to teach them about responsibility, and with love enough to help them celebrate the triumphs, our children's self-concept will grow each time they survive on their own.

I AM WHAT I THINK YOU THINK I AM

Unfortunately, many parents don't give their children a chance to build a positive self-concept—they concentrate on their children's weaknesses. They reason (often unknowingly), "Before my Jackie can be motivated to learn anything, she has to know how weak she is." Whenever these parents talk to their children, the conversation centers on what the children are doing poorly or what they can't do. If a child has trouble with fractions, or has sloppy work habits, or doesn't pronounce syllables properly—whatever the problem—the parents let him or her know about these weaknesses continually. The result is a constant eroding of their child's self-concept.

But parents who build on their kids' strengths find their children growing in responsibility almost daily.

Think of how we, as adults, respond to a person who builds on our strengths. If somebody very important to us thinks we're the greatest thing since remote-control channel changers, we will perform like gang-busters for that person. But if that important person thinks we're the scum of the earth, we will probably never prove him wrong.

It's the same way with kids. Kids say to themselves, "I don't become what you *think* I can, and I don't become what I think I can. I become what I think you think I can." Then they spend most of their emotional energy looking for proof that what they think is our perception of them is correct. For example, long before my (Jim's) son Charlie developed his writing skills, his seventh-grade teacher raved about his writing potential, building him up and encouraging him. Responding to what his teacher thought he could do, Charlie worked on his writing with determination and enthusiasm and is now an accomplished writer.

As parents, we play an integral part in the building of a positive self-concept in our children. In our words and in our actions, in how we encourage and how we model — the messages we give to our kids shape the way they feel about themselves.

THE THREE-LEGGED TABLE

The building of a person's self-concept can be compared to building a three-legged table. Such a table will stand only when all three supports are strong. If any one of the legs is weak, the table will wobble and rock. If a leg is missing, goodbye table.

Our children's three-legged table of self-concept is built through the implied messages we give. These messages either build them up and allow them to succeed by themselves or add to childhood discouragement and reduced self-esteem.

Unfortunately, many of the really powerful messages we send to our children have negative covert meanings. We may mean well, but the words we use and the way we phrase them are received by the children as something totally different from what we meant to say. This is one of the severe tragedies of parent-child relationships.

LOVE-AND-LOGIC TIP 3
A Tale of Self-Concept

The first day of kindergarten. Big school. Big bus. Big moment in a child's life. Susan and Sam — two very different kinds of kids — walk through the school doors on that very big first day. In Susan's head the thinking goes, "School's probably going to be fun. I'll get a fair shot. I can learn. School is really no big deal."

In Sam's head the music is not so harmonious: "School may not be that great. I may not be able to learn. I may have a hard time with friends. I really don't know about this school business."

A child's self-concept is deeply entrenched by the time that child hits kindergarten, built through the many implied messages he or she received during the first few years of life. From the moment of birth, a child embarks on a lifelong mission of feeling accepted and being noticed in a positive way.

Susan picked up all kinds of positive messages during her first five years. Messages that she was capable, lovable, and valuable. Her parents sent signals that said, "We love you the way you are, because you are you." At a very early age, Susan was given opportunities to do her own thinking. The decisions were about elementary issues, true, but they were decisions nonetheless. Her parents asked things like, "Do you want to wear your coat today, or do you want to carry it?"

Sam picked up messages, too. But those messages told him he was not measuring up to parental expectations. The messages he heard said, "We could have a lot more love for you if you would just do better." Sam was never allowed to decide anything. When it came time to put on his coat, his parents said, "You get that coat on. You're not going out without it."

On that first big day of school, Susan had very few doubts about her ability. But Sam was filled with questions, misgivings, and lack of confidence.

When the first assignment sheet was passed out, Susan jumped right on it and gave it her best shot. She had a go-for-it attitude. But Sam held back. He stalled. He needed encouragement. A voice inside his head said, "You may not do as well as the others. Watch out! You're going to be hurt." Sam didn't want to look bad so he avoided completing — or even starting — his work.

By sixth grade Susan will probably have continued in success, every small victory building on an already healthy self-concept. But Sam will probably be apathetic, not caring about anything, avoiding all challenges and making life miserable for his parents and teachers.

Building a child's self-concept begins at home, and it begins from the moment of birth.

For example, a simple question like, "What are you doing that for?" packs a double meaning. The overt message seems like a simple question. However, what our child hears underneath is, "You're not very competent." When we say, "If I've told you once, I've told you a thousand times," the implication is, "You're pretty dumb, and your neurons work sluggishly."

Such implied messages are putdowns, the kind of messages that would make us fighting mad. We can lace these messages with as much syrup as the human voice is capable of carrying — "Now, *honey,* you're not going without your coat today, are you?" — but the implied message still shines through; namely, "You're not smart enough to know whether or not your own body is hot or cold." The ultimate implied message says, "I'm bigger than you are. I'm more powerful than you are. I have more authority, and I can make you do things." A current bumper sticker sums this up nicely: "Because *I* said so, that's why."

Whenever we order our children to "Shut up!" "Stop arguing!" or "Turn off the television!" we're sending a message that slashes into their self-concept. Why is this? Because, when we give children orders, we are saying:

- ◆ "You don't take suggestions."
- ◆ "You can't figure out the answer for yourself."
- ◆ "You have to be told what to do by a voice outside your head."

Conversely, when we parent with love and logic, we emphasize a powerful combination: letting our children fail in non-threatening situations while emphasizing their strengths. We must be uncritical and nonprotective. Parents who raise irresponsible children do exactly the opposite! They're critical *and* protective.

A good rule of thumb in knowing how to speak to a child is to ask yourself, "What would I say and how would

I say it if I were giving a similar message to my boss at work?" No doubt, bosses sometimes do dumb things, but it's amazing how clever we can be in "correcting their behavior" without insulting their character.

LOVE-AND-LOGIC TIP 4
What We Say Is Not Always What Kids Hear
Kids are quick to understand the underlying messages we give, whether they come through our words or our actions. Each of the following examples carries an overt as well as a covert meaning.

"George, I'll let you decide that for yourself."
OVERT MESSAGE: "You can decide."
COVERT MESSAGE: "You are capable."

"June, I'll give you one more chance, but you better shape up."
OVERT MESSAGE: "Things better improve."
COVERT MESSAGE: "You can't handle it. I have to provide
    another chance."

"Why in the world did you do that, Lee?"
OVERT MESSAGE: A simple question.
COVERT MESSAGE: "That was very foolish."

"Don't go out without your coat, Tessa."
OVERT MESSAGE: A simple reminder.
COVERT MESSAGE: "You're not capable of thinking for
    yourself."

Leg One: I Am Loved by the Magic People in My Life
The best kind of love is the love that comes with no strings attached. Our love for our children must never be conditional. This is not easy, but the benefits are enormous. Genuine love must be shown regardless of the kids' accomplishments. That does not mean, however, that we approve of all of their actions.

All too often, parents don't give their kids the chance to experience their love. Some withhold love as a way of making children behave better or to break bad habits. Others, in their zeal to help youngsters improve schoolwork, for example, exert so much "love" getting them to do their homework that the children receive covert messages that real love will have to wait until they improve. These parents express their love through intensity and pressure. They forget the real signs of love (eye contact, smiles, etc.); and the kids, very tuned in to nonverbal communication, see this and think their parents' love depends on their achievement in school.

In reality the interaction between parents and children — the expression of love — is far more important than the kids' successes or failures. Here's another paradox: *Kids can't get better until we prove to them, beyond a shadow of a doubt, that they're good enough the way they are.*

Strong, effective parents say in both their covert and overt messages, "There's a lot of love here for you regardless of the way you act or do your work at school or anyplace else." When this love is combined with touching, a smile, and eye contact, a super-glue bond is created between parent and child. Children never get too old for this experience. (How do you feel when someone treats you this way?) Such a combination packs powerful messages. Kids remember these messages for a lifetime when they come from the "magical people" in their lives — close family members and special teachers. They subconsciously — even consciously — set out to prove that their magical people are correct.

Leg Two: I Have the Skills I Need to Make It
To build children's self-concept parents must send messages that tell the children they have the skills people their age need to be successful. Each child must feel that he or she can compete with other kids in the classroom, on the ball field, at home — anywhere kids interact. Children must know that within themselves are the necessary ingredients to handle life. Dad can't make it for them. Mom can't make them successful. They alone have the abilities to succeed.

These skills are learned through modeling. Good parental models help children develop good attitudes and feelings about themselves. To be good models, parents must realize that children are always watching them and taking cues on how to act and react. Wise parents think, "Don't get too uptight if our children don't always listen to us—but tremble in fear that they see what we do."

LOVE-AND-LOGIC TIP 5
Messages that Lock in Love
A lot of hugs, wrestling, friendly pushing and shoving, and even playful punching all forge a strong bond between parents and children. Blend these with smiles and eye contact. Use these emotional times to lock in implied messages such as:

- ◆ "You do a great job of thinking for yourself."
- ◆ "You are always a good helper when I need you."
- ◆ "There's always a lot of love here regardless of what happens."
- ◆ "It looks as if you will always be able to solve your own problems."
- ◆ "I bet you feel good when you do such a nice job."

Kids are born with a great capacity to learn to do things the way big people do. They observe and attempt to copy what they see. Their prime interest is learning and doing things just like their parents do them. All too often, however, parents discourage their kids with the model they present.

Timmy sees his dad sweeping the garage. He grabs a little broom and starts moving dirt around, imitating his father. Inside, Timmy is thinking, "I feel big. I am learning how to use the broom. I hope Dad notices."

Dad notices all right. He notices all the spots the little tyke is missing, rather than appreciating the learning that is taking place. "*Timmy*," he says, his voice dripping with disapproval, "look at the mess you're making! Please go play and let me finish this."

If Dad pulls this once in a while (we all do), Timmy's

self-concept will come out of it unscathed. But habitual discouragement will lead to a poor self-concept in the child. He'll stop trying to imitate responsible "adult" behavior.

Parents who routinely focus on the end result rather than on the learning taking place wind up with kids who have a negative self-concept about their skills. Then parents wonder, "Why don't our kids ever want to help around the house?"

"But what about quality control?" you may be asking. When do we start worrying about the end results? We don't want unswept dust piles in the garage forever, do we? The quality of learning improves with practice, encouragement, and modeling. Say, "Gee, Timmy, you really know how to sweep. Isn't it fun to do a good job? Watch how I use the broom and get all of the dirt." This gives the child a good model to copy. Like Dad, Timmy wants to do a good job and feel good about it, too.

When children are small, we can teach them a great combination: *getting the job done, fun,* and *me.* We make sure that getting the job done is fun. We model that. *We never pass judgment on the work of children when they are trying to learn.* Rather, we say things like these:

- "I can see that you are working hard to learn to do long division. Let me know if you would like some help."
- "I see that you are learning to make the bed just like Mommy. Would you like me to show you how I (not *you*) get the wrinkles out?"

Whenever possible, we slip a little fun in the task. When my (Foster's) children were small and we did the dishes together, we imagined the unhappiness of the germs on the dishes as we rinsed them off before putting them into the dishwasher. "What's going on here?" the germs would scream. "What's that big rag doing? It's wiping me off the plate. Argh-h-h-h!" Then, as the plates were put in the dish-washer, the germs continued their dialogue: "What's this big round room? What's going on in here? Hey, guys, it's starting to spin. We're all going to get killed! Argh-h-h-h!" When my children were high school age, they were still imagining the germs screaming and dying.

It would have been easy to come down on them when they were little for missing a spot here and there, but that would have spoiled the fun.

As our children grow up, we remove ourselves from the triad, and they are left with the job and fun. We are elsewhere, having fun doing our own jobs.

Leg Three: I Am Capable of Taking Control of My Life

Children with a strong third leg on the three-legged table listen to a little voice in their head that says, "I am capable of taking control of my life. I can make decisions, and I am strong enough to live with the good and the bad conse-quences of my decisions." Children who say this have been allowed to make decisions about the things that affect them directly.

Many parents *tell* their children they expect them to be responsible for themselves, yet these same parents are for-ever informing their kids when they are hot, cold, hungry, thirsty, tired, or even when they need to go to the bathroom. We've all heard these messages:

- ◆ "Put on your coat. It's too cold for you to be going out without it."
- ◆ "You *can't* be hungry. We just ate an hour ago."
- ◆ "Sit down and be quiet. You don't need another drink."
- ◆ "You get to sleep right this minute!"
- ◆ "Be sure to use the bathroom before we leave."

Each of these messages tells children they are not

capable of thinking for themselves, that they cannot take control of their life and make decisions. Interestingly, such messages often come from parents who moan and groan about their kids' lack of responsibility and ability to think for themselves.

LOVE-AND-LOGIC TIP 6
What They See Is What They Learn

I (Jim) spent my childhood on the wrong side of the tracks, in a trailer in industrial Denver. When my family scraped enough money together, we bought a little garage to live in while my dad built a house on the property.

Dad worked a morning shift downtown, rode the streetcar to work, and when he returned at 2:00 p.m. every day, he picked up his hammer and saw and built a house. It took seven years.

As I watched him work, I thought, "Wow, he gets to do all the fun stuff. Mix the concrete, lay the bricks, put on the shingles, hammer nails, saw wood." I watched it all day every day.

At the end of the day, when my dad knocked off, he invariably said, "Jim, clean up this mess." So I would roll out the wheelbarrow, pick up a shovel and a rake, and clean up the mess. At the same time, Dad would explain to me that people have to learn to clean up after themselves. They need to finish and put the tools away.

When my dad noticed that I left my own stuff laying around, he complained, "Why don't you ever pick up your stuff, Jim? There's your bike on the sidewalk, and your tools are all over the place. When you go to look for a tool, you won't know where it is." I, of course, was learning all about cleaning up. I was learning that adults *don't* clean up after themselves.

Had my father modeled by cleaning up after himself—saying in the process, "I feel good now that the day's work is finished, but I'll feel better when I clean up this mess and put all the tools in the right places"—he would have developed a son who liked to clean up his own messes. As it is, my garage is a mess to this very day.

Although kids are born with great courage to take control of their own lives and make decisions, they have little experience on which to base their decisions. So they often make poor choices. But they can learn from those mistakes, provided parents don't get too involved.

LOVE-AND-LOGIC TIP 7
It Can Be a Cold World Out There
It was a frigid Colorado evening. One of those Jack London nights when spittle freezes before it hits the ground. My (Foster's) family was heading out on an errand. Gathered at the door, my wife asked our son, "Andrew, do you want to wear your coat?"

He said, "No, I don't need my coat." He was wearing a T-shirt.

Modeling responsible adult behavior, my wife said, "I'm sure glad I'm wearing my coat," then she put on her coat, and the family got into the car.

Two blocks from home, muffled sounds came drifting from the back seat — the unmistakable sounds of shivering and teeth chattering. My wife said, "Do I detect goose bumps in the back seat?"

"Y-y-eah-h-h!" Andrew stuttered. The next words spoken were some of the wisest ever to pass from Andrew's lips: "N-n-n-ext time, I'm g-g-g-oing to wear my c-c-c-oat!"

"Oh, honey, that sounds like a good idea." (Our drive lasted long enough for the message to sink in but not so long that Andrew turned blue.)

Had my wife said, "Wear your coat. It's cold out," Andrew would have probably said, "No." And she would have said, "I'm your mother, wear your coat."

Then, Andrew would have been sitting in the back seat, warm as toast, hating her, and not learning a thing. He would have been thinking, "Okay, I'll wear my coat, but only because you made me. Just wait until I'm old enough to decide myself about wearing a coat!"

When little kids rebel, parents can quash the rebellion with a stern order and get good short-term results. But when kids hit adolescence and rebel, parental orders become unenforceable.

Allowing children at a young age to practice decision making on simple issues teaches them to think, to control their own lives. When adolescence hits, they will be less susceptible to peer pressure on booze, drugs, sex, and other temptations. They will have learned that they can make their own wise decisions. Those kids can become their parents' very best friends during the tough teenage years. They can also become their own best friend.

IF WE'RE HAPPY, THEY'RE HAPPY

You may find this an extremely distressing thought, but kids learn nearly every interpersonal activity by modeling. And you know who are their primary models, don't you? The way they handle fighting, frustration, solving problems, getting along with other people, language, posture, movements — everything is learned by watching the big people in their lives. From learning to talk to learning to drive, their all-seeing eyes are scoping out our actions.

By the time children are toilet trained, they're dressing up in Mom's shoes or wearing Dad's hat. If Mom's at the sink doing dishes, there they are too, splashing around — getting totally soaked. If Dad's under the hood tinkering with the carburetor, there the kids are, lending their own "helping" hand. Many parents get irritated — it's a bother, they're under foot. But what learning opportunities — at low price tags!

The key to parental modeling may sound strange to you. It goes like this: *I always model responsible, healthy adult behavior by taking good care of myself.*

The second greatest commandment tells us to love our neighbors as we love *ourselves.* The old saying, "We can't love somebody else unless we love ourselves" applies here. If we, who know ourselves best, love ourselves little, it's hardly likely that our neighbors will be overjoyed with our presence.

However, true self-love is always an enlightened self-love. That is, taking care of ourselves really means taking care of our brother, too. After World War I, with Germany in chaos, the seeds for World War II were set. We didn't care for our German brothers. After World War II we truly helped the Japanese, and World War III has not yet occurred, nearly fifty years later.

In reality, there is no prolonged win-lose position for any of us. It either has to be win-win or lose-lose. Only in the short run is it possible to have win-lose situations.

In spite of the second greatest commandment, the maxim of taking good care of ourselves — even putting ourselves first — may go against our parental grain. Many parents believe their kids should always come first. No sacrifice is too great. These parents are taxi driver, delivery service, alarm clock, travel agent, and financial analyst, all at the same time. You hear them say, "Yes, it's a bit inconvenient for me to drop everything and cart you down to that kindergarten transactional analysis seminar, but I will, because I love you and always put you first."

However, children growing up with this arrangement see that the parents are not taking care of themselves in a healthy way. They're always putting the children first and themselves last. Kids, who learn everything through modeling, will put themselves last as well.

When high school rolls around, these same parents will wonder why their children have such a poor self-image. After all, they say, "I always put them first. I always did everything for them." In reality, young people with a poor self-image are following their parental model. In a self-destructive way, they're putting themselves last.

Of course, as parents we never put ourselves first at the expense of our children. We don't want the children to lose out. We want them to win. But we want to win as well. Thus we always strive for a win-win situation. We want to feel good, and we want our children to feel good. So we take care of ourselves in a nice, healthy way.

We still take our children places, we still do things for them. But most of the time we do so because it also contributes to our sense of well being. We so enjoy taking our son to his soccer games because we enjoy the chatter in the back seat and the chance for him to excel in athletics. We like ferrying our daughter to her music lesson because it makes us feel good to hear her musical progress. Most of life is a growing, enjoyable experience—for *both* of us. And *what we gain is nothing compared to what the child gains.*

4
CHILDREN'S MISTAKES ARE
THEIR OPPORTUNITIES

◆

How much better to get wisdom
than gold!
To get understanding is
to be chosen rather than silver.
PROVERBS 16:16

Jack and Sarah had a big problem with ten-year-old Eric. Everything they told Eric to do, he did. Whether it was chores, studying hard, getting along with others, showing respect for adults and teachers — Eric came through flawlessly.

Eric got up on his own every day. He always stacked his school stuff neatly by the door before strolling to breakfast, and he always gave himself enough time to enjoy his meal at a leisurely pace. He never walked out without his lunch, assignments, gym clothes, permission slips, or anything else. He consistently reached the bus stop five minutes early. At school he rarely got into trouble. His teachers liked him; he had lots of friends. When he hopped off the bus in the afternoon, he jumped right into his chores and his homework without being told. At the first evening yawn, he decided to turn in for the night—often a good half-hour before required. One Saturday morning the kid cleaned out the garage before Jack and Sarah even got out of bed!

Some parents would kill for such "problems" with their kids. But Jack and Sarah sat up at night worrying about Eric. "He might go through his childhood years with very few opportunities to grow from his mistakes," they reasoned.

Fortunately, most of us don't "suffer" from Jack and Sarah's problem. Our kids mess up plenty. As they do, they will have more than enough chances to grow in responsibility as they resolve their problems.

LOVE-AND-LOGIC TIP 8
Responsible Kids, Irresponsible Kids
The most responsible kids I (Jim) encountered in my three decades in education were the kids at an inner-city school where I served as an assistant principal. They all hailed from federally funded housing projects. Those kids woke up in the morning without an alarm clock and got to school in time for breakfast without any assistance from their parents.

They knew that if they got there, they got breakfast; if they didn't, they missed it. They never missed a bus when it was going someplace they wanted to go.

The most irresponsible kids I ever saw were in an upper-middle-class suburban school. The first day of school a thousand kids arrived in eighteen different buses. Half of these kids ran straight to the playground for some pre-bell frolic. The other half raced directly to the principal's office to phone their folks for forgotten registration materials, coats, and lunches.

Responsible behavior has a direct correlation to the number of decisions children are forced to make. The more they make, the more responsible they become.

MOTHER, PLEASE, I'D RATHER DO IT MYSELF

Oftentimes we impede our kids' growth. We put ourselves exactly where we shouldn't be—in the middle of their problems. Parents who take on their kids' problems do them a great disservice. They rob their children of the chance to grow in responsibility, and they actually foster further irresponsible behavior.

The greatest gift we can give children is the knowledge that with God's help they can always look first to themselves for the answers to their problems. Kids who develop an attitude that says, "I can probably find my own solutions," become survivors. They have an edge in learning, relating to others, and making their way in the world. That's because *the best solution to any problem lives within the skin of the person who owns the problem.*

When we solve problems for our kids — the ones they could handle on their own — they're never quite satisfied. Our solution is never quite good enough. When we tell our kids what to do, deep down they say, "I can think for myself," so oftentimes they do the exact opposite of what we want them to do.

Our anger doesn't help either. Certainly, it galls us to no end when our kids mess up something in their own lives. When they lose schoolbooks or bring home failing grades, it's only natural for us to explode in a living, breathing Fourth of July display. But anytime we explode at children for something they do to themselves, we only make the problem worse. We give kids the message that the actual, logical consequence of messing up is making adults mad. The children get angry in return, rather than learning a lesson from the consequences of their mistake.

When we intrude into our children's problems with anger or a rescue mission, we make their problems our problems. And children who know their problems are the concern of their parents don't worry about them. This can be explained partly by the "no sense in both of us worrying about it" syndrome. Most of us don't worry about something if somebody else will do the worrying for us.

Before I (Jim) met Shirley, I harbored a great dislike for going to the gas station, simply because I hated to part with the money. The only thing that forced me to visit the pumps was a near-empty reading on the fuel gauge.

However, when I married Shirley, she discovered this habit of mine and, fearful that I would run out of gas, she took on the responsibility of either reminding me to fill the tank or filling it herself. I never had to worry about it; she had my problem well in hand.

After a while, though, Shirley got tired of my irresponsibility and stopped rescuing me. One night I ran out of gas, walked down a dark road for help, stepped off a bridge, and tumbled ten feet into a stream bed. I was laid up for eight weeks before I walked again. It was then that I realized that she was willing to worry about how much gas was in her car, but unwilling to worry about mine. Guess who has never run out of gas since? If Shirley wasn't going to worry about that, somebody had better—me.

Kids who deal directly with their own problems are moved to solve them. They know if they don't, nobody will. Not their parents, not their teachers—nobody. And on a subconscious level, they feel much better about themselves when they handle their own problems.

YOU HAVE YOUR TROUBLES, I HAVE MINE

The list of kids' problems is endless. Getting to school on time, getting to school at all, dropping out of school, being hassled by friends, hassling friends, harassing teachers, being harassed by teachers, poor grades, laziness, wrong choice of friends, drugs, alcohol, and many, many more—all are problems kids have to face. The major combatants in these problems are the child and others, or the child and himself or herself. Parents who involve themselves in all of these problems can spend their every waking hour at the task. *These parents unfortunately believe they show their love for their children by jumping into these conflicts and rescuing them.*

Even when a kid doesn't seem concerned about his or

her problems, we should stay out. A child's laziness, for example, is still a child's problem. While unwillingness to do homework, bad grades, or tardiness at school may be maddening to us, we must find a loving way to allow the consequences to do the teaching for the child, whatever those consequences might be. (Many specific problems are discussed in part two, "Love-and-Logic Parenting Pearls.")

LOVE-AND-LOGIC TIP 9
When to Step in, When to Stay out of Kids' Problems
Occasionally, we should make our children's problems our problems: (1) we step in when our children are in definite danger of losing life or limb, or of making a decision that could affect them for a lifetime; and (2) we step in when the children know that we know that they know that they cannot cope with their problem, and the consequences are very significant.

For instance, in a rare circumstance, parents might insist that their child change classrooms. This should only happen if the child is suffering so greatly that the entire school future could be threatened, and when the child knows that he or she is in a losing situation. For as soon as the parent steps in, the child gets the "you can't cope" message. Sometimes, though, we don't care if the child gets that message because everyone already knows it.

Remember: *Everything we fix for our kids, our kids will be unable to fix for themselves.* If Anna has trouble on the school bus and we haul on down to the stop one morning to talk to the driver and the other kids, Anna is robbed of any chance of handling that problem by herself, and will believe that she can't.

If there's more than a ten percent chance that our child might be able to work it out, we should keep clear of the problem.

Or consider children's friends—often only parents see this as a problem. One parent said, "When Jeff thinks his crummy friends are swell, *he* doesn't have a problem over it." Of course, he *does* have a problem—he just doesn't see it. With time, though, he will. Surprisingly, children usually see their problems sooner if we allow them to *reach their own conclusions.*

On the other hand, some of the children's behaviors *are*

our problems. If the problem is how our children relate to us (disrespectful talk, sassing, etc.), how they do chores, playing loud music, waking us up in the middle of the night, misbehaving when in public, or matters surrounding their life support system (bread and butter, room and board), then the problem has drifted out of their domain and directly into ours. In short, *if it's a problem for us, it should soon be a problem for them.*

If Ricky shoots off his mouth at school, we let the teachers take care of the consequences with our support. But if Ricky shoots his mouth off at us, we deal with it.

If Maria's slowness in getting ready for school makes her late, we stay clear of the problem. But if Maria's slowness in getting ready to leave the house makes *us* late, we deal with it.

If Oscar's room is a nationally declared disaster area, we let him wallow in the mire. But if Oscar trashes the living room within fifteen seconds of arrival, that affects us and we help him handle it—our way.

Again, we are modeling appropriate adult behavior. We don't allow other people to harm us, and we therefore raise children who know how to care for themselves and, as teens and older, won't allow others to cause them problems.

PROBLEM, PROBLEM, WHO OWNS THE PROBLEM?

Unfortunately, separating the kids' problems from our problems is not always as cut and dried as we would like. The line between the two often becomes blurred by parental indecision, guilt, insecurity, and importantly, our own childhood's authoritarianism.

When our guilt or indecision moves us to step into our children's problems, we cater more to our own emotions than to the children's needs. However, most kids want us to understand *their* feelings, not sooth our own emotional turmoil by offering them solutions.

LOVE-AND-LOGIC TIP 10

If It's a Problem for Us, It Should Soon Become a Problem for Them

"Where's Snuggles?" The question from Sandy, a seven-year-old girl, was frantic with concern. Sandy missed the excited yelping when she got off the bus. She missed the afternoon throw-and-retrieve game. When she investigated further, she found her dog was nowhere to be seen.

"I've taken Snuggles to her new home at Betty's place," Sandy's mother said.

"To Betty's house?" asked Sandy.

"Right," Mom said. "But there's bad news and good news. The bad news is that Betty already is falling in love with Snuggles and may never want to give her up. The good news is that Betty gave us three days to decide if Snuggles can come back here."

"Snuggles is at Betty's house!?" Sandy screamed. "Why?"

"Well, frankly," Mom said, "I got tired of seeing Snuggles' ribs showing. I don't like looking at skinny, malnourished dogs that are being abused. Their whining hassles my ears and their ribs disturb my eyeballs. So, Snuggles needed a new home."

"B-b-b-but, how do I get Snuggles back?" Sandy stammered. "Will you take me to Betty's house?"

"You must be kidding," Mom said flatly. "I just took the dog over there. Now I'm supposed to bring her back? Do I look like an idiot?"

So Sandy phoned a neighbor who happened to drive near Betty's house on his way to work. (Kids can be very resourceful when they have to be.) Mom had phoned the neighbor earlier in the day to explain what might happen.

"Sure, I'll take you by there on my way to work," the neighbor said. "And I'll pick you and Snuggles up on my way home. You'll have to call Betty and see if you can spend the day at her house."

"Oh, I will," Sandy gushed. "I will."

Snuggles is safe at home now, happy, loved, appreciated — and well-fed. Sandy learned an important lesson about responsibility.

I (Foster) sometimes worry that this approach sounds too tough, taking the pet out of the home with the possibility it may never return. But I also know that life offers tough consequences. The message we want to convey to our children is that neglecting responsibilities presents serious consequences. Poor personal health habits, for example, can lead to illness and ultimately to death. Children need to learn that lesson. The question is this: Will they learn it on goldfish or hamsters or dogs, or on themselves?

This is tough on us. Our guilt nags us; our insecurity bugs us to death. What will our friends think when our son is the jerk of his school? How will we be viewed at church when it's our daughter who never knows the name of the boy who slew Goliath? How can parents who love their child stand back and watch him or her blow it time and time again without stepping in with help?

Our intervention into our children's problems demonstrates a selfish love. We must rise up in a higher love—a love that shows itself in allowing our children to learn on their own.

Standing at her kitchen window, Martha watches son Bobby slug neighbor boy Matt, after which Matt, unhurt, flees home in tears. Is this an obvious child's problem? Of course it is. If Martha allows her own emotions to control her reaction, she can rob Bobby of the chance to grow in responsibility.

If she reacts with embarrassment—"What will people think?"—Bobby receives the message that she doesn't care about how *he* feels. She cares only about how others feel.

If his mother is angry and authoritarian—"Don't do that! Apologize to Matt!"—Bobby will rebel. Parents who make a child do something their way find that the child tries all the harder to do it his or her way.

If Martha throws up her hands in helplessness—"What will I ever do with you?"—she assumes ownership of the problem. Bobby will probably think, "I don't know, but *you* figure it out."

Each of these possible responses is based on Martha's own emotions. Each denies Bobby the chance to tackle his own problem. It would be better for Martha to focus on Bobby. She could either say nothing, or offer her ear for listening if Bobby wants to talk about it. Or if she is so troubled she feels she must express her disapproval, she could say, "Bobby, I saw what you did to Matt. Do you approve of that? What would be the right thing to do now?

How do you think Matt feels? I hope next time you'll find a better way to solve that kind of problem." Such comments put the burden of resolving the problem as well as the future response on Bobby's shoulders.

What should Martha do if Matt's mother, Joan, comes over—spitting nails? How would she keep this Bobby's problem? If that happens, it is best for Martha to say, "Well, Joan, I can understand your being upset. If my son had been hit, I'd be upset too. I think it would be great for you to tell Bobby exactly how you feel. In fact, I'll call him down and you can talk to him now."

Martha must emphasize to Joan that she cannot control her son's behavior when he is away from home. On the other hand, she understands if Matt is angry and wants to hit Bobby back. Martha tells Joan that she will let Bobby know that this threat is a distinct possibility, and that such consequences would be sad for *him*.

Throughout this whole episode, Martha should realize that Joan may not be helping her son Matt by moving in and taking care of Matt's problems. On the other hand, she also realizes it might help Bobby a lot to let him know that the neighbors are upset and will not let him get away with such an act.

Allowing children to solve their own problems presumes an implicit, basic trust that their behavior will change as they learn from their experiences—when they learn that hitting another person usually results in bad news for the provocateur.

To repeat: *The best solution to any problem lies within the skin of the person who owns the problem.*

5
SETTING LIMITS
THROUGH THINKING WORDS

❖

Rash words are like sword thrusts,
but the tongue of the wise brings healing.
PROVERBS 12:18

L ove-and-logic parenting is a law-and-order philosophy. Just because we recommend that parents shy
away from issuing orders and don't impose their
solutions on their kids' problems, does not mean we give
license to all sorts of misbehavior. Nothing could be further from the truth. Neither of us is in any way soft on
misbehavior.

True, we allow our kids to mess up, and we don't drive
home the lesson of their misdeeds with our words. We are
slow to lecture; we never actually *tell* our kids what they
have just learned.

We believe telling our kids what to think is counter-
productive. We can give them guidance (more on that in
subsequent chapters), but they must think for themselves.

LOVE-AND-LOGIC TIP 11
Using Love and Logic with Toddlers
Notice that parenting with love and logic advocates setting really
strong limits and boundaries in toddlerhood. How does this square
with our advice to allow children to fail and to be slow to give
orders? Actually, it squares exactly because the limits we set for
toddlers always involve (1) modeling good adult behavior by
caring for ourselves, and (2) life or death issues. As we have noted,
in both of these instances the child's problem does become our
problem. Let's look at an example.

Two toddlers, "Thoughtful" and "Thug," want to be picked
up. They raise their hands and scream demandingly at their
parents. Thug's parents pick him up. In essence, they say, "Be
obnoxious with me and you'll get your way."

However, when Thoughtful raises her hands and screams, her
father politely says, without anger or sarcasm, "Thoughtful, why
don't you lie down on the linoleum? I can't pick you up when you
act like that." Thoughtful learns right away to say, "Daddy, will
you pick me up, please?"

The boundaries we set for our children are in reality the
boundaries we set for ourselves. The more squishy and indecisive
we are about our own boundaries, the more soggy and inconsistent
we are about the limits we set for our toddlers.

The earlier they start, the better. When our children leave
our care, we want them to be so good at thinking that they
can face the bigger problems and the daily hassles of life
with competence and good sense.

So, if we don't order our kids around, how *do* we talk
to them? How do we set limits on their behavior without
telling them what to do? Limits are crucial to love-and-logic
parenting. Our kids need the security in which they can
begin making those all-important decisions. They have to
know the boundaries.

BUILDING WALLS THAT DON'T CRUMBLE

Imagine yourself plopped down on a chair in a strange,
totally dark environment. You can't see your hand in front
of your face. Your only security is the chair. You don't know

if you're on a cliff, in a cave, in a room, or wherever.

Eventually you muster enough nerve to move away from the chair and check your immediate surroundings. You find four solid walls. What a relief! Now you feel a little more secure and safe enough to begin exploring the rest of the room, knowing that you won't fall off the edge.

But what if you tested the walls and they crumbled? You would move quickly back to your chair for security. And there you would stay. Your entire environment is mysterious and threatening.

Now imagine what it is like for newborn babies. They pop out of the cozy, comfortable, familiar surroundings of the womb into a totally unknown, alien world. Their world is like the dark room. Babies crawl out seeking limits on their behavior, they seek security in knowing what they can and cannot do.

Beginning in infancy, we set limits for our kids, limits that put boundaries around their behavior. How fast do we bolt from our interrupted deep sleep to tend to wailing Wally in his crib? Do we permit little Janet to wage pabulum war from the high chair? Is Terry allowed to slap Mommy when he's mad? Can Suzie make our every shopping expedition a walk on the wild side?

Some parents build walls in the form of firm limits for their children; others leave their kids to feel insecure and afraid by providing few limits, or limits that crumble easily.

I (Foster) once counseled a young mother who had a unique problem with her son Burt: The boy ate coins. He was a walking slot machine. Pennies. Nickels. Dimes. Not many quarters. And *no* half dollars. She was thankful for that, but it was still a problem.

Burt would start to swallow a nickel, and Mom would make like a Samoan pearl diver trying to dig it out. "I tell him not to, but I can't make him stop," she wailed. "What am I going to do?"

I found out during our conversation that they lived on a

busy Denver thoroughfare, so I asked the mom, "Does Burt run out onto Wadsworth Boulevard?"

The mom said, "Well, of course not. On *that* I mean business."

One limit was firm, the other soft. Burt knew playing in traffic was a no-no. But when it came to eating coins, *bon appetit.*

Kids seem most secure around parents who are strong, who don't allow the limits they place on their kids to crumble. Children lose respect for adults who cannot set limits and make them stick. Kids who misbehave without having to face the consequences become brats.

Children lucky enough to have limits placed on them in loving ways become secure enough not only to deal effectively with their own emotions, but to form satisfying relationships with others.

These limits allow children to develop self-confidence. As a result, they're easier to teach, they spend less time misbehaving, and they grow up to be responsible adults. When we don't provide firm limits, our kids suffer from low self-esteem. And when they have low self-esteem, they behave accordingly.

HOW TO TALK TO A CHILD

For many parents setting limits means issuing commands, and backing up those limits with more commands spiced with sternness and anger. They figure every time they say something to their kids they're setting limits, and the louder their voice gets, the firmer the limits become. They may get results with their orders, but they're setting their kids up for a fight (against them) and doing them a great disservice at the same time.

You've probably noticed that there's something different in how love-and-logic parents talk to kids. *We're always asking questions. We're always offering choices.* We don't tell our kids what to do, but we put the burden of decision making on their shoulders. As they grow older, we don't tell them what the limits are, but we establish limits by offering choices.

LOVE-AND-LOGIC TIP 12
Thinking Words and Fighting Words
Observe the difference between some fighting and thinking words:

◆ Child says something loud and unkind to the parents:
FIGHTING WORDS: "Don't you talk to me in that tone of voice!"
THINKING WORDS: "You sound upset. I'll be glad to listen when your voice is as soft as mine is."

◆ Child is dawdling with her homework:
FIGHTING WORDS: "You get to work on your studying!"
THINKING WORDS: "Feel free to join us for some television when your studying is done."

◆ Two kids are fighting:
FIGHTING WORDS: "Be nice to each other. Quit fighting."
THINKING WORDS: "You guys are welcome to come back as soon as you work that out."

◆ Child won't do his chores:
FIGHTING WORDS: "I want that lawn cut, *now!*"
THINKING WORDS: "I'll be taking you to your soccer game as soon as the lawn is cut."

Love-and-logic parents insist on respect and obedience, just as command-oriented parents do. But when love-and-logic parents talk to their children, they take a different approach. Instead of the fighting words of command-oriented parents, they use *thinking words.*

Thinking words—used in question form—are one of the keys to parenting with love and logic. They place the responsibility for thinking and decision making on the children. They help kids do exactly what we want them to do—*think.* As much as possible.

Children learn better from what they tell themselves than from what we tell them. They may do what we order them to do, but their motivation for obedience comes from a voice other than their own — ours. Kids believe something that comes from inside their own heads. *When they choose an option, they do the thinking, they make the choice, and the lesson sticks with them.* That's why, from early childhood on, parents must always be asking thinking-word questions: "Would you rather carry your coat or wear it?" "Would you rather put your boots on now or in the car?" "Would you rather play nicely in front of the television or be noisy in your room?"

We don't use fighting words: "You put that coat on now!" "Because *I* said put your boots on, that's why! It's snowing outside." "I'm trying to watch this football game. So *be quiet!*"

The difference between thinking words and fighting words often may be subtle — after all, the limit in each case is the same — but the child's reaction is usually different.

Kids fight against commands. They see an implied threat in them. When we tell them to do something, they see our words as an attempt to take control of the situation. Anytime we usurp more control, it means that they have less control. They exert themselves to regain the control they see slipping away.

THE THREAT CYCLE

The temptation is oh so great. We desperately want to assail our kids with commands and threats to limit their behavior. The reasons are simple: (1) using threats doesn't make us feel like the wimp we feel like if we whimper, cry, beg, or plead with our kids; and (2) threats sometimes work.

In my (Jim's) early years as a teacher, I frequently used threats to motivate students to do their work. To one student I would say, "You get that work done or you're not going to lunch," and the kid's pencil became an instantaneous cyclone of activity. To another I would say the same thing, and the kid would say, "Who cares?"

Some kids respond to threats, some don't. They may do as they're told, but they're angry at the person who gave

---

LOVE-AND-LOGIC TIP 13
Eat Nicely Here, or Play on the Floor

Dinner time with two-year-old Danny—Mommy and Daddy and Baby, too. Talking over the day's events. Listening to the little tyke's new words and new experiences. A cozy scene for family bonding and love, right? That's how Mom and Dad see it. But Danny has different ideas.

First, the bread crust is hurled into Dad's soup, splashing the Christmas tie. Then the little fists are sledgehammering the sliced-up wieners on his tray. Next he's on his feet trying to climb out the back of the highchair. Then the top is off his safety cup, and he's anointing Fido with milk. All of which is punctuated with intermittent blood-curdling screams that would make a band of pillaging Huns proud.

Mom and Dad have a problem. They must convince this child that such dinner behavior is unacceptable. They must set limits.

They could slap his little hands, grab his little shoulders, and peer directly into his little eyes while saying, "Danny eat nice, or Daddy spanks." And Danny would show them just how strong his little lungs are.

Or they could say, "Danny, would you like to eat nicely in the chair, or would you like to play on the floor?" Notice that the parents do not ask Danny to "play nicely" on the floor. We can't make a child play nicely on the floor, but we can help them to eat nicely. One thing is under our control, the other is not.

Fighting words or thinking words. With one, Mom and Dad have done all of the thinking, and the meal is chaos. With the other, they let Danny do some thinking, and order is restored.

The parents have shown Danny how they make themselves happy by taking care of themselves, and Danny can decide about his own happiness.

If Danny chooses the floor, he will learn soon enough that it's a long, hunger-filled time until breakfast. And the limits for behavior at the dinner table will be firmly set in his mind—if a little boy shall not be nice, neither shall he eat. All this is accomplished with no anger, no threats, no fighting words.

Too bad about the Christmas tie.

the order. Or they may perform the task in a way that is unsatisfactory, simply to regain some of the control they had taken from them. In either case, they're breaking the limit we're trying to set.

Passive-Aggressive Behavior

When children are commanded to do something they don't like, they often respond with passive-aggressive behavior. Kids know they must comply with the order, or reap punishment if they don't. They channel their anger in a way that will hurt their parents — so subtly that the parents don't know they're being hurt. They'll make it sting sharply enough so that those parents will think twice before asking those kids to do that chore again, for example.

Traci was assigned to do the dishes, something she ranked on her happy-meter right up there with letting dentists drill her teeth. She used every conceivable trick to get out of it. Sometimes she was able to put it off past her bedtime. Then all of a sudden, she became very mature about her need for the good old eight-hours-a-night: "You're always telling me I need my sleep," she'd say. "I'll do them in the morning." When morning came, of course, she was running late and had to rush for the bus. There the dishes sat, still unwashed. Eventually Mom did them because they were stinking up the kitchen.

But Mom decided to get tough one night and said to Traci, "I want those dishes washed now! I'm tired of you wasting all evening in front of that television while those dishes sit there."

"Oh, all right," Traci replied. "I'll do it." She walked to the sink and washed with such enthusiasm and gusto that she "accidentally" dropped one of Mom's best glasses. It shattered on the floor.

"Oh, I'm sorry, Mom," she said when Mom raced into the room. "I was trying so hard. I wanted to do a good job."

Mom is between a rock and a hard place. How could Mom punish a girl who was trying so hard?

Traci's passive-aggressive behavior told her mom an important message: You'll think twice before you make me do the dishes again. Mom might conclude, "What's the use? It's easier to do it myself than to go through all this."

Passive-Resistive Behavior
When kids react to parental demands with passive-resistive behavior, they resist without telling the parent they are resisting. The resistance is in their actions, not their words. It happens whenever a parent tells a child to do something, to which the child responds by claiming he or she forgot the request or with less than instantaneous obedience.

One of Harold's teachers ordered, "Get down the hall to your class, young man, and get there right away." Harold "got" down the hall, all right, but at a speed imperceptible to the human eye.

The teacher said, "Hurry up, Harold."

"Hey, I'm going," Harold replied. "I'm doing what you told me. How come you're always on my case? How come you're always hassling me?"

Harold was attempting to wrest back some control of the situation. He was fighting. "I'll go," he said inside. "But I won't go your way, I'll go my way."

A sure sign of passive-resistant behavior in children is prolonged parental frustration. Certainly, parents may be frustrated without having passive-resistant children, but *all* passive-resistant children have frustrated parents.

WE'D RATHER THEY THINK THAN FIGHT

Fighting words invite disobedience. When we use them, we draw a line in the sand and dare our kids to cross it. They will fight the limits we impose when we use fighting words. Fighting words include three types of commands:

♦ When we tell our kids what to do—"You get to work on that lawn right now."
♦ When we tell our kids what we will not allow—"You're not going to talk to me that way!"
♦ When we tell our kids what we *won't* do for them—"I'm not letting you out of this house until you clean the living room."

LOVE-AND-LOGIC TIP 14
Let Your Yes Be Yes, and Your No Be Yes, Too
The word *no* is one of the biggest fighting words in the parental arsenal of commands. It is a child's call to arms, a shot across his bow. Kids hear it far too often. In fact, parents of two-year-olds are known to say no—in some form or other—seventy-seven percent of the time. Children quietly tire of hearing it. In fact, they hear it so much that the first word many children learn to say is *no* and variations of *no.*

When kids hear *no,* half the time they ignore it. They hear it so much that sometimes they think it means "maybe," other times they think it really means "yes."

The rule with *no* is that we use it as seldom as possible. But when we use it, we mean business. All of the other times we are tempted to use *no,* we can avoid a fight by forcing our kids to do the thinking, by replacing *no* with a *yes* to something else. In this way, we use thinking words instead of fighting words, and we establish the behavior we want. Compare the two:

FIGHTING WORDS: "No, you can't go out to play until you practice your lessons."
THINKING WORDS: "Yes, you may go out to play as soon as you practice your lessons."

FIGHTING WORDS: "No, you can't watch television until your chores are done."
THINKING WORDS: "Yes, you may watch television as soon as your chores are done."

When we issue such commands we are calling our kids to battle, and in many cases these are battles we cannot win. Why not bypass these hassles and make our words ones that cannot be fought? Why not steer away from commands?

Our limits can be set much more effectively when we're not fighting with our kids. It has been clinically proven that kids who are thinking cannot fight us at the same time.

Love-and-logic parents make statements with *thinking words,* telling our kids:

- ♦ What we will allow — "Feel free to join us for your next meal as soon as the lawn is mowed."
- ♦ What we will do — "I'll be glad to read you a story as soon as you've finished your bath."
- ♦ What we will provide — "You may eat what is served, or you may wait and see if the next meal appeals to you more."

Our kids have little chance to fight these statements. They're too busy thinking about the choices they have been given and the consequences that may result from their choice.

By using thinking words, we are able to set limits on our children's behavior without telling them what to do. For instance, if we want the lawn mowed before they eat their next meal, we set that limit by offering them a choice: of mowing the lawn and eating, or of not doing the lawn and not eating.

Now, of course, when offered such choices our children will probably say, "That's not fair! Why should I have to take either of those choices?" The answer lies in the fact that our choices must always make "real world" sense (we'll explore this more in chapter 6). So, we would lovingly say to our child, "Well, honey, that's the way the world works for me. First, I get my job done, then I get paid, then I eat. If it's good enough for me, who do you think I think it's also good enough for?" The child will always answer, a little dejectedly but insightfully, "Me." And we always respond with, "Good thinking."

When we give our children the right to make decisions,

there is no anger for them to rebel against. Nobody's doing their thinking for them, and the limit is established.

MEAN WHAT YOU SAY, AND SAY WHAT YOU MEAN

Just as quickly as kids learn where the limits are, they'll test them. In fact, they *need* to test them in order to assure themselves that the limits are firm enough to provide the needed security. They need to find out if we mean what we say, if we're going to stand firm on our word or not.

Most children seem to have their own special testing routine. Some use anger, others guilt, some are sneaky, and others feign forgetfulness as a means of testing parental resolve. They never seem to say, "Thanks, Dad, I feel a lot more secure now that I know you mean what you say. I appreciate your loving me enough to set these limits." Instead, they pout, complain, stomp around, run to their rooms, whine, or talk back.

Kids are not above laying guilt trips on us either. If we tell them to get the job done before they next eat, they'll respond with "Imagine being raised by a dad who doesn't even let me eat around this place!"

They'll do anything to make us back off. But we must stand firm. After all, the limit that was imposed was the children's choice. Of course they're hungry if they decided to put off their next meal because they didn't mow the lawn. That hunger is the consequence of their action.

We are certainly empathetic with their hunger. We know how it feels to miss a meal, and we tell them so in all kindness and understanding, "It is a bummer to miss a meal. Any of us would feel hungry. But, boy, do I ever enjoy the next meal."

If we relent, we demolish the meaning of those consequences. We set up a crumbling limit for our children. If we get angry at them for the choice they made — or if we rail into them with "I-told-you-so's" — we also present a crumbling limit. Those children then have ample reason to direct their anger toward us, instead of toward themselves.

Thinking words, giving choices, displaying no anger — these are the ingredients for establishing firm limits with our kids.

6
GAINING CONTROL THROUGH CHOICES

❖

Hear, my child, and accept my words,
that the years of your life may be many.
PROVERBS 4:10

"Calling Luke to dinner is like calling the cat," Marna said. "He doesn't even flinch when I talk to him.

"He spends all his time at his computer. One night, I said to him, 'Come to dinner,' and do you think he'd come? He never even looked up. So I said, louder, 'Come to dinner!' Again nothing happened.

"So I said, 'I mean it!' Luke just kept punching away. I am so frustrated! How can I be a good mother if I can't make my kid do what I want him to do, when I want him to do it?"

Many of us share Marna's frustration and her concept of parenting. We don't feel like good parents unless we can run our kids around like little robots.

It all boils down to control. We want to control our

children. We want them to do what we want them to do, when we want them to do it. At times our kids fight us with a passion. Before we know it, we're locked into a control struggle.

How much easier it would have been for Marna to use thinking words, whispered into her son's ears: "We'll be serving dinner for the next twenty minutes, and we'd love to have you join us because we love eating with you. We hope you make it. But if not, just catch us at breakfast." But no, Marna couldn't do that. Nor can many of us. When we do it, we don't feel like we're in control.

PARENTING JUST GETS MORE AND MORE CURIOUS

Control is a curious thing. The more we give away, the more we gain. Parents who attempt to take all the control from their children end up losing the control they sought to begin with. These parents invite their children to fight to get control back.

In the battle for control, we should *never take any more than we absolutely must have*; we must always cut our kids in on the action. When we do that, we put them in control on our terms. We must give our children the control we don't need to keep the control we do.

This battle for control begins early in life. From infancy on, children live a drama of gaining responsibility and control over their own lives. Little Karen wants to make decisions; she wants to think for herself.

Giving even the smallest children a certain amount of freedom and control over their lives instills in them the sense of responsibility and maturity we want them to have. Independence helps children learn about the real world as their wisdom grows from the results of their decisions.

However, there is a downside. We can give our kids too much control, and kids with too much control are not pleasant to be around. In fact, they don't even like to be around themselves. They're brats. These children need to be controlled; their behavior indicates they'd be happier if they were controlled. Yet they demand more control with their pouts and tantrums. Control is power. Having received at least some degree of control very early in life, they always seek more.

LOVE-AND-LOGIC TIP 15
You'll Do What I Tell You to Do

Jan, the mother of twelve-year-old Amy, parents in the "do what I tell you to do" style. Jan thinks she should be in control of everything in her daughter's life. She controls when Amy gets up, when she goes to bed, what kinds of clothes she wears, who her friends are supposed to be, what grades she is supposed to get, and how much television she watches.

Parents like Jan, when they come home from a night out, don't rush to hug their kids and say, "We missed you." They run to the television set and hug *it*, to see if it's still warm from being on when it was supposed to be off!

Kids will take this stuff for a while, but eventually they shake off this blanket-like control. One day Amy said to herself, "Mom is getting out of line. It's about time to reel her in. Maybe it's time for her to get a C- on the report card." Amy received the C-, and Jan came unglued. She ranted, raved, grounded, withheld, lectured, yelled at the teachers, and recruited her husband to deliver his "get good grades now or you'll never cut it in college" speech.

Amy sat back and thought, "You haven't seen anything yet. Wait until Mom gets an F."

Poor Jan. She has yet to discover that kids get report cards; parents don't. Jan cannot make her daughter learn. Jan actually *loses* control over Amy with every ounce of effort she pours into her quest for controlling her. It's one of the many battles Jan, and all parents, will eventually lose.

The battles we can't win are those that center on children's brain activity. If kids can hook us into trying to make them talk, think, learn, or go to sleep at a certain time, they've got us. We'll never win those battles, and moreover, we'll expend needed energy fighting them—energy that can be effectively channeled into battles we *can* win.

When parents pull in the reins, these children resist and are filled with anger. Kids who start with too much power force us to tighten the limits around them — and that makes them angry. Adults are no different. When control in some area of life is reduced, we also react to the tightening of the reins with anger. We feel that what is rightfully ours has been stripped away.

THE RIGHT DOSE OF CONTROL

What, then, is the right amount of control to give children? Psychologist Sylvia B. Rimm, Ph.D., says people of all ages compare the amount of control they have in a relationship only to the amount of control they used to have — not to the amount they feel they should have. When more control is allotted with time, people are satisfied; when control is cut back, people are angry. Thus children who grow up with parents who dole out control in increasing amounts are usually satisfied with the level of control. It's always more than it used to be.[1]

Rimm's analysis is called the "V" of love. The sides of the "V" represent firm limits within which the child may make decisions and live with the consequences. The bottom of the "V" represents birth, while the top represents the time when the child leaves home for adult life.

When kids are very little, love-and-logic parents will give away control in certain areas. While giving the tyke a bath, the love-and-logic dad will say, "Do you want to get out of the tub now, or do you want to stay in a few more minutes?" Dad doesn't need that control. Or at the table, Mom might say, "Have you had enough milk, or would you like some more?" Mom gives that control to the child.

Thus toddlers make decisions about things like chocolate or white milk; ten-year-olds decide how to spend their allowances; and seventeen-year-olds make decisions on nearly every aspect of their lives. Children's control over their lives is ever-expanding.

Unfortunately, many parents invert the "V." They treat

LOVE-AND-LOGIC TIP 16
The "V" of Love
In the "V" of Love, the limits we set down for our kids' behavior are ever-expanding, offering more and more freedom as the years go by. Unfortunately, many parents do the opposite (the inverted "V"). They grant many privileges when the children are young and then find themselves taking control away from their kids. The result is unhappy children.

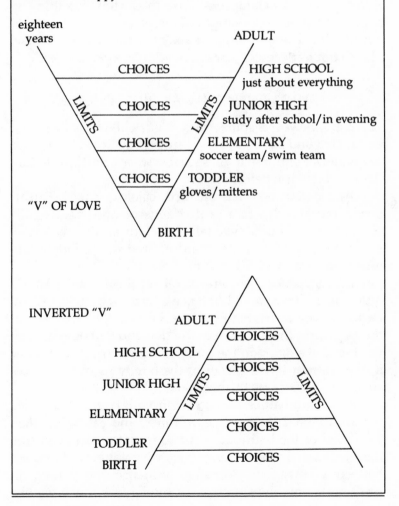

their kids like miniature adults right from the start, with all the privileges of adulthood granted immediately at birth. These children soon become tyrants. Their parents don't control them; they control their parents, holding them hostage with temper tantrums and pouts. More tragically, many children who begin life with too much power eventually lead unhappy lives as they grow older. Misbehavior early in life forces parents to clamp down on them, thus resulting in anger and rebellion as rights and privileges are forcibly withdrawn. These unhappy youngsters are forever crying, "Life's not fair! You're always treating me like a child."

WAGING WINNABLE WAR WITH CHOICES

There are, however, some areas of our children's lives that remain beyond our control and are best avoided. If we exert our will over children in these areas, we are destined to fail. And we blow it when we try.

Any parent who has pleaded, cajoled, bribed, threatened, contorted his face grotesquely, or done headstands trying to make a little tyke talk for relatives, already knows about these sorts of control battles. Brett isn't going to talk unless *he* wants to. The same goes for the battle of the pureed vegetables. We can force-feed them down Diane's little gullet all we want, but if she doesn't want to eat them, back out they come. And we lose. Ditto at the other end of the gastrointestinal tract. We may demand that our children do their dirty work on the potty chair, but before we know it, they're over in the corner of the family room with faces sporting an ominous flushed look.

These are battles we can't win with commands. They pertain to what children learn, think, and eat, when they go to bed or the bathroom, and so forth. In each, children fight tenaciously to win, and when we get involved in these battles, we invariably lose. We influence our children in these areas only by *modeling*. We model how much we like *our* food at the table. We talk, in self-referenced comments, about how good it makes us feel to clean up *our* plate, to eat *our* vegetables. But every time we issue demands, we invite a fight—and eventually we lose.

The secret to establishing control is to *concentrate on fighting battles that we know we can win.* That means we must select the issues very carefully. We must pick areas where we *do* have control over our kids. Then we must offer choices in those areas.

We may not be able to make Christy eat when she's at the table—that's an unwinnable battle—but we can control whether she's at the table or not. We may not be able to control when Bruce does his chores, but we can make sure he does them before he eats his next meal. We may not be able to control the disrespectful words that pop out of Shanna's mouth, but we can make sure she doesn't use them in our presence—we send her away until she can speak reasonably with us. (More on these specific issues in part two, "Love-and-Logic Parenting Pearls.")

We cannot afford to demand blind obedience to our every wish. When faced with such demands, kids dig in their heels and hold out for their own values—and that's a control battle we'll lose every time.

LOVE-AND-LOGIC TIP 17
Three Rules for Control Battles
1. Avoid a control battle at all costs.
2. If you're going to get into one, win at all costs.
3. Pick the issue carefully. Whenever we lose a control battle, it's because we have not chosen the issue carefully.

Choices Change All

Winnable war is waged through choices, not demands. Choices change the entire complexion of the control struggle. They allow us to give away the control we don't need and gain the control we do. With choices kids have no demands to react against, and the control we need is established.

One parent said, "As soon as I give my three-year-old a choice, everything changes. It works every time. I see a complete personality change in Kari when she has a choice—when I change my words from fighting words to thinking words. I'm still setting the limit and I'm still getting what I want, but I'm eliminating the fighting."

Why Choices Work
One reason choices work is that they create situations in which children are forced to think. Kids are given options to ponder, courses of action to choose. *They must decide.*

Second, choices provide opportunities for children to make mistakes and learn from the consequences. With every wrong choice the children make, the punishment comes, not from us, but from the world around them. Then children don't get angry at us; they get angry at themselves.

Another reason choices work is because they help us avoid getting into control battles with our children.

Finally, choices provide our children with opportunities to hear that we trust their thinking abilities, thus building their self-confidence and the relationship between us and them.

Dealing with choices and being held responsible for their own decisions, prepare youngsters for the lifetime of decision making that awaits them in adulthood. Effective parents, however, should offer choices only when they are willing to ensure that their children will be forced to live with the consequences.

THE BAD BOY IN BURGER KING:
A CASE STUDY ON WINNING A CONTROL BATTLE

How then do we take control of a situation when our children are determined to battle us every step of the way?

The following story sheds light on waging a winnable war with kids.

Six-year-old Marty was a master at goading his folks into unwinnable control battles. Picture him seated in a fast-food restaurant booth with Mom and Dad. They are all slurping up the last of their soft drinks and gathering their things to leave for some shopping before the mall closes.

All except for Marty. He's blowing bubbles through his Coke straw, playing airplane with his french fries, and his teeth have no more than nibbled the edges of his hamburger bun.

Mom, her face resembling a technicolor explosion, says through gritted teeth, "Hurry up with that thing! We've got shopping to do."

Marty responds by buzzing his hamburger with a fry. He's heavy into everything but eating. Now Dad jumps into the fray: "Can't you do something with that kid?" he asks his wife. "K-Mart will be closed by the time we get out of here."

Mom grabs Marty's burger and tries to guide it into the child's face. But Marty is not buying into the "open wide for the airplane" bit. His jaws clamp shut like a bear trap.

Next come the threats: "You hurry up with that thing, or you know what's going to happen to you? We'll go shopping without you and leave you here."

Marty picks up his burger and holds it about two feet from his face, as if there is at least a mathematical possibility that he might comply with the parental order.

Soon, almost imperceptibly, the corners of his mouth begin to tighten into a curt, self-satisfied smile. Dad sees it. He jumps out of the booth and yells, "Okay, that's it! We're going shopping without you, and do you know what's going to happen to you, buddy? Cops are going to come get you!"

Suddenly, Marty's hamburger flops down on the table.

Marty, no doubt, is thinking something like this: "Look at me. I'm only six years old, and I've totally controlled these two adults for twenty minutes without even opening my mouth. What a power trip! I control their tone of voice, the color of their faces, and whether or not they make fools of themselves in public. The last thing on my mind is worrying about being picked up by cops."

Who's Controlling Whom?

Marty's parents blew it entirely in trying to make him eat his food. Marty had total control over what went down his food pipe. Had his parents offered him choices instead of making demands—had they taken only as much control as they absolutely needed—they would have been able to put Marty in control on their terms. But how?

Two Ways to Leave with Me: Hungry or Not Hungry

A love-and-logic parent would say, with a smile on his or her face, "No problem, Marty. My car will be leaving in five minutes. There are two ways to leave with me: Hungry is one way; not hungry is the other."

That gives the parent as much control as he needs. He doesn't need to control whether the burger goes down the child's throat—in fact, he can't control that. But he can control when the car leaves.

By offering Marty the choices, the struggle is transferred inside Marty's head. Marty's too busy to argue—he's weighing his choices, "Hungry . . . not hungry. . . . Hungry . . . not hungry"—and Dad and Mom have five minutes of welcome tranquility. They gain control by relinquishing control.

However, many parents, after issuing the alternatives, would be tempted to harp and nag while the child is making up his mind. They would say things like, "Don't forget, my car is leaving in three minutes. If you don't eat that food, you're going to be hungry. You'll wake up in the middle of the night, and there won't be anything to eat. It's going to be a miserable night."

These sorts of reminders are putdowns. Cut the kid some slack. Marty's smart enough to remember the choices he's been given.

LOVE-AND-LOGIC TIP 18
No Problem
The phrase "no problem" is a lifesaver for the parent confronted with a misbehaving child. When Mom or Dad says it, even the dumbest kid in the world can figure out what it means: No problem for the adult, big problem for the kid. When we say "no problem," we give ourselves a few precious seconds to come up with thinking words that will inform our children what we will do, not what they have to do.

Under Your Power or Under My Power

When Marty's five minutes are up, Dad would then enforce this child's choice. He could use fighting words like, "You get in my car," but much better would be thinking words like, "My car is leaving now."

Probably Marty will say, "Yeah, but I'm not finished."

Once again Dad would offer Marty choices: "No problem, son. You can go under your own power, or my power. Either one," followed by ten seconds for Marty to decide. The point Marty must understand is that the car's leaving doesn't depend on whether or not he's done eating. The car is leaving — period.

Assuming Marty decides not to come with Dad willingly — a reasonable assumption, by the way — then Dad must pick Marty up and head for the door with him. (An important note on choices: There are always three. In this example, Marty can do it one way, or he can do it the other way. The third option is that the parent will decide. Marty didn't decide, so his dad decided for him.)

A lot of parents are bothered by what comes next. After all, it is unlikely Marty will look into Dad's eyes and coo, "Great parenting style, Dad." No, he will probably be kicking and screaming like a banshee. Everybody in Burger King will be watching every move Dad makes as he hauls this wild, flailing kid out the door.

Let them watch. First, the people in the restaurant aren't saying to themselves, "Look what a bad parent that guy is." They're thinking, "Thank goodness, that's not *my* kid. Now I can eat in peace." Second, parents of six-year-olds don't go into a place like Burger King to build lasting relationships with the other people dining there. So, who cares what they think? And third, teaching a child responsibility is not a free ride. We must steel ourselves for resistance and opposition. There's a price we must pay.

Keep the Parental Trap Buttoned
To ensure that Marty has a learning experience from this incident, his mom and dad must remember one thing: To keep their mouths shut. Save the words for happy times. The only time to reason with a child is when both parties are happy. Parents who consequence their child with their mouths moving strip the consequence of its value. Allow the consequence to do the teaching.

Carrying the kicking and screaming Marty out the restaurant door, Dad would then put him very gently in the car and drive off, all the while keeping mum about the incident. Before the evening is over, Marty will probably say something very intelligent—to wit, "I'm hungry."

When he says it, Dad should stifle the temptation to get angry and say, "Sure, you're hungry. I try to tell you these things, but you never listen. That'll teach you to eat your hamburger in the restaurant." Such a response only engenders more antagonism and resistance in the child.

Dad should administer the consequences with a compassionate sadness. For example: "Oh, for sure, son. That's what happens to me when I miss my dinner. I'll bet you'll be anxious for breakfast. Don't worry. We'll cook a good one."

Without doubt, Marty will learn more from this response than from anger and threats. Sorrow and consequences and an arm around his shoulder, are powerful learning agents.

LOVE-AND-LOGIC TIP 19
The Brain Drain

Children are going to fight the choices we give them. Rare are the kids who will always choose one of the given choices and happily go on with life. Sometimes, they'll fight with a vengeance.

One of children's favorite ploys is "Brain Drain." In "Brain Drain" they attempt to make us do the thinking, thus draining our brains of energy. Guilt, indecision, telling us we don't love them — they'll lay anything on us that comes to mind with words such as, "That's not fair," "You don't love me," and the like. Every time they do this, we are forced to drain our energy tank in supplying justification for the choices we give them.

However, if anyone is going to drain anyone's brain, let it be us draining our children's brain. We do this by holding firm to our choices. Observe the following scenario:

ROY: "Hey, Dad, bye. I'll see ya. I'm going out with Jason."
DAD: "Hold on, Roy, I think you promised you'd have the garage swept by this morning before you did anything else."
ROY: "But I don't have time right now, Dad."
DAD: "That may be so, son, and feel free to go as soon as you sweep the garage."
ROY: "Aw, c'mon. I promised my friends I'd go."
DAD: "I'm sure that's true, Roy, *and* feel free to go as soon as you sweep the garage."
ROY: "I'll do it when I get back. Jason does his chores after he plays."
DAD: "I'm sure that's true, Roy, *and* feel free to go as soon as you sweep the garage."

Repeat the choices over and over again. Don't get angry. Stick to your guns, and your brain will remain refreshingly full.

Most kids will get frustrated with this after three or four tries, thinking, "How quickly can I get out of this crazy situation?" Out loud they will say, "I know. . . . Don't say it again."

CHOOSE YOUR CHOICES CAREFULLY

Many well-meaning parents who offer choices to their children err in their delivery of those choices. Often they offer their children two choices — one the adults can live with, and one the adults cannot live with.

For example, had Marty's dad, in Burger King, said, "You either eat that or you stay here," Marty probably would have decided to hang around until the place closed for the evening. Kids have a way of finding the jugular in any conflict.

The art of offering choices can be distilled to two basic points:

1. Never give more than two verbal choices, but make sure the child knows that there is an implied third choice: If he doesn't decide, then we'll decide for him.
2. Make sure whichever choice the child chooses, it will be something we can live with.

A Caution on Giving Choices
Be mindful that it is easy to turn the choices into threats that tell the youngster, "Choose my way or else." When we say to our child, "You can either clean your room or lose your right to watch television," it is no different from our boss saying to us, "Would you rather do that report today or get fired?" We must offer real choices, not threats:

- "Would you rather clean your room or rake the lawn so I'll have time to clean your room?"
- "Would you rather clean your room this morning or this afternoon?"
- "Would you rather pick up your toys or hire me to do it?"
- "Do you want to spend your allowance on fun things

this week or pay someone to do your chores?"
- "Do you guys want to settle the problem yourselves or draw straws to see who sits by the car window?"

Non-threatening choices, offered in a calm, non-hysterical manner, give children a chance to take some control over their problems.

Rules for Giving Choices
In summary, as we offer choices to our kids, we should remember five basic points:

1. Always be sure to select choices that you as a parent like. Never provide one you like and one you don't, because the child will usually select the one you don't like.
2. Never give a choice unless you are willing to allow the child to experience the consequences of that choice.
3. Never give choices when the child is in danger.
4. Never give choices unless you are willing to make the choice in the event the child doesn't.
5. Your delivery is important. Try to start your sentence with one of the following:
   "You're welcome to _____ or _____."
   "Feel free to _____ or _____."
   "Would you rather _____ or _____?"
   "What would be best for you—_____ or _____?"

NOTE
1. Sylvia B. Rimm, Ph.D., *How to Parent So Children Will Learn* (Watertown, Wis.: Apple Publishing, Co., 1990).

7

THE RECIPE FOR SUCCESS:
EMPATHY
WITH CONSEQUENCES

---❖---

My child, if your heart is wise,
my heart too will be glad.
PROVERBS 23:15

I (Jim) had a problem some years back with my kids going to bed on time. I've often said, "If I had a dollar for every time I shouted at my kids, 'You guys get in that bed right now and go to sleep!' I'd be relaxing at my summer home in the Bahamas right now."

As a concerned parent, I knew that lack of sleep would make the next day miserable for my kids. They'd drag around, unable to think clearly or perform well at school. Why, they might even fall asleep at their desks! That seemed too high a price for my kids to pay. So I kept badgering them to go to sleep on time, threatening to spank them, to take away television privileges, to take them out of sports, or anything else I thought might work.

One day a great truth of parenting was revealed to me:

You can't make a child go to sleep.

I marched upstairs, called my kids together, and said, "Kids, I've got to apologize. I've been meddling in your life. I've been trying to tell you things you should be deciding on your own. So, I'm going to get out of this, and if you can remember two simple little rules, I'll never hassle you again about going to sleep. Think you can handle that?"

"Yeah," they said, "we can handle that."

"Rule one," I said, "is that from eight o'clock on is private time for your mom and me. We don't want to see or hear you, but feel free to be awake. Rule number two: We all get up at six o'clock every morning. See you at six o'clock." I gave them each a little kiss and went back to the family room.

At 10:30 p.m. the lights in both my kids' rooms were still on. Attempting to provide them with an admirable model to emulate, I wandered into their rooms and said, "Well, I'm going to bed. I don't want to be grouchy in the morning. See you then."

When I got up at 6:00 a.m., the lights were still blazing away. One child was sleeping with his clothes on; another had come to rest in a sitting position in the corner. I then discovered another great truth of parenting: It's a lot easier to wake kids up than to put them to sleep. Turning two radios up to front-row Rolling Stones concert decibel level takes hardly any energy at all.

Three bleary-eyed and moaning kids wandered around the house that morning, rubbing their eyes and whining, "I'm too tired to go to school today," "I'm sick, Dad," and "I want to go back to bed."

I didn't get angry at them. Instead I felt genuine sadness for their plight. "Well, for sure, kids," I said, "that's what happens to me too when I stay up too late. I bet it's going to be a long day at school. Well, try to have as good a day as you possibly can, under the circumstances. We'll see you when you get home. Have a nice day."

I watched them tramp to the bus stop. At 3:30 p.m. the bus pulled up on the return trip and from its door staggered little six-and-a-half-year-old Charlie, who wearily traipsed up the stairs and found his bed. There he slept the rest of the afternoon with his baseball hat crunched down over his nose, his heavy jacket still on, and his tundra boots laced up to his knees.

At dinner that night, Charlie kept nodding off in his plate. However, before the meal was completed, he said a most intelligent thing: "I think I'll go to bed early."

It took Charlie one night to learn a lesson I had spent years trying to teach him. And it happened because I was empathetic and allowed the consequences to do the teaching.

HURTING FROM THE INSIDE OUT

Had I paddled my kids or taken away television privileges, I wouldn't have been nearly as effective in teaching my kids the lesson about the importance of a good night's sleep. I would have been using punishment, and the *real* world by and large *doesn't operate on punishment.*

Imagine yourself banging a fender in the parking lot at work. You feel bad about it, and when you come home that evening, you explain the accident to your spouse. "What!" your loving mate shrieks. "That really makes me mad. You know how you wanted to go skiing this weekend? Well, forget it. You're grounded!"

A ridiculous scenario? Of course. As adults we don't get grounded when we mess up in life; nobody washes our mouths out with soap when we swear. Punishments don't happen in the real world unless crimes are committed. When people are punished for something, they seldom pause for self-examination. Resentment is the more common reaction.

The same holds true for children. When we send kids

to bed early because they sassed us, we are doling out punishment. When children tote home all Ds and Fs on a report card and we rescind television privileges for two months, we are not allowing the consequences of mistakes to do the teaching.

LOVE-AND-LOGIC TIP 20
Warning: Good Parents Don't Give Warnings
Think of yourself as tooling down the freeway at 70 mph in a 55 mph zone. You see the multicolored lights of doom blinking in your rear-view mirror, and you think of one thing, and one thing only: "I'm going to get a ticket."

The cop saunters up to your car, nice as can be, writes the ticket, bids you adieu, and is on his merry way. He offers no hysterics, no anger, no threats. Just courtesy and a little slip of paper—the consequences of your breaking the law.

As an adult, you would never think, in your wildest imaginings, of telling him, "I'll be good, officer. Honest, I won't speed anymore," and having him say, "Well, okay. If you'll be good, I won't write you a ticket." That is the stuff of fantasy. But how often in our homes is our kids' pleading met with parental shilly-shallying?

Little Richie is a terror at the table. He pouts and complains and whines and builds miniature motocross courses on his plate around which he pushes peas up and down ramps of celery stalks and around mini-mountains of mashed potatoes.

Mom, thinking she's consequential, says, "Okay, Richie, your dinner's over. Off to your room."

Richie says, "I'll be good."

And what does Mom say but, "Oh, well, okay. Are you sure you'll be good? Or are you going to keep goofing off at the table?"

"No, I won't do it anymore. I'll be good."

"Well, okay," Mom says, thinking her problems are over. "You can stay."

The real world doesn't operate on the multiple-warning system, and neither should we. Parents who give a lot of warnings raise kids who don't behave until they've had a lot of warnings.

The real world operates on consequences. If we do a consistently lousy job at work, our boss doesn't take away our VCR. He fires us.

When we punish our children we provide them with a

great escape valve, an escape from the consequences of their action. They never have to think when they're punished. They don't have to change their behavior. They think, "I'm being punished for what I did. I'm doing my time." And their anger is directed toward the punisher — us.

As love-and-logic parents we want our kids to *hurt from the inside out*. This happens when we allow the consequences to do the teaching. Consequences leave kids thinking very hard about their behavior and their responsibilities. Consequences lead to self-examination and thought.

NATURALLY OCCURRING CONSEQUENCES

The best consequences are those that fall naturally. If Teresa is a nuisance at the dinner table and chooses to play on the floor rather than eating nicely at the table, then it only makes sense that she'll be hungry at bedtime. If Greg continually neglects his school work and brings home failing grades, then retention to the same class-level makes sense.

Naturally falling consequences allow the cause and effect of our children's actions to register in their brains. When they ask themselves, "Who is making me hurt like this?" their only answer is, "Me."

But these consequences put a painful, sinking feeling into our stomachs as parents. They're exactly the things we don't want to happen to our children.

Brian gets cold when he doesn't wear his jacket. Sheila gets hungry when she goes to bed without eating. We are tempted to remind them of the pain of cold, the misery of hunger. But if we want the consequences to do their work effectively, we cannot afford to take that luxury.

David, age eleven, was a sleepyhead. Every morning he'd beat to death the snooze alarm on his bedside clock. Seven o'clock, then 7:10, then 7:20, and every time the jarring clang of his alarm rattled his ears, his fist would promptly pound on the snooze button, and he'd be back off in dreamland.

LOVE-AND-LOGIC TIP 21
A Real-World Bus Service
When Paul, age twelve, first came into our (Foster's) home as a foster son, we knew he was passive resistant and would have trouble being on time. His "thing" was being late. Therefore, during his first week with us, to help him grow we arranged a learning experience for him.

He wanted to be dropped off in town and meet us at a grocery store about ten miles from our mountain home. I told Paul I would be glad to drop him off in town and that I could meet him at the grocery store at 5:00 p.m. Then I added, "Paul, I operate like the bus service does in the real world. However, I'm a little bit more lenient. I will wait three minutes. If you are at the grocery store between 5:00 and 5:03, I'll pick you up. If for some reason you can't make that time, don't worry. I'll swing back past and wait from 10:00 to 10:03. If, due to poor planning, you can't make it then, don't worry. I'll swing by at 7:00 tomorrow morning on my way to work. I'll wait from 7:00 to 7:03."

Well, I knew Paul would test me, and he did. When I went at 5:00, no Paul. When I went at 10:00, I waited three minutes then started to drive away, and out of the shadows as I was pulling off, runs Paul. He was waving his arms wildly over his head shouting in the night, "Here I am, here I am! Don't leave me!" I think that little episode had a definite beneficial effect, and although Paul had been chronically late for his parents, he was never late for us.

Mom quickly tired of this every-morning hassle, and she decided to let the consequences teach her son a lesson. One day when David roared downstairs twenty minutes before school was to start, warmly yet firmly she said, "Oh, glad to see you're up. What do you think you'll do today in your room?"

"In my room?" David said. "I'm going to school!"

"Well, that's good," Mom said. "How are you going to get there? The bus left ten minutes ago."

"You're going to take me, of course," David replied.

"Oh, sorry," Mom said. "I can't do that. I'll be busy with my housework all day. Feel free to arrange other transportation, or to spend the rest of the day in your room so I can do my work without any interruptions, just like other school days.

"When lunch time comes, feel free to make something for yourself," Mom continued. "And if I go on any errands this afternoon, I'll take care of getting a baby-sitter for you. But don't worry if you can't pay the sitter. You can pay me back later in the week, or I can take it out of your allowance. But you only have to worry about that if I have to go out on an errand. So it's not a problem right now.

"Have a nice day, David. I'll see you at 3:30 when you normally get home on the bus."

Of course, when the next morning rolls around and David wants an excuse note, Mom will say, "Oh, I can understand that. I know how nice a note is to explain why you were absent from school. But you know I only write notes for you when you're sick. Hope it works out okay with your teacher, though. Have a nice day, under the circumstances."

There's no question—doing this takes guts! But the reward of changed behavior is worth it. These consequences all fall naturally, and they fit the "crime" of not getting up in time for school. David misses school; he's out of his mom's hair just like any other school day; and he doesn't get a note.

Amazingly, kids never seem to miss two days of school in a row with this technique. Without the company of others and without the attention of a parent who nags them, they become conspicuously unhappy.

IMPOSING CONSEQUENCES

While naturally occurring consequences are best, occasionally our children's actions don't lend themselves to such consequences. In those cases, we must impose the consequences ourselves.

The art of arranging consequences comes naturally to some parents, while others must gain this type of expertise through practice. Often parents choose to impose consequences that are irrelevant, or if relevant, the consequences are either too harsh or too lenient.

LOVE-AND-LOGIC TIP 22
Empathy, Not Anger
Letting the consequences do the teaching isn't enough. We as parents must show our empathy — our sincere, loving concern — when the consequences hit. That's what drives the lesson home with our children without making them feel we're not "on their side." Consider the following examples:

- Aaron misses dinner because he didn't do his chores
  on time:
  ANGRY WORDS: "Of course, you're hungry! I bet you
    won't do that again. I told you you'd be hungry."
  EMPATHETIC WORDS: "I know how that feels, son.
    I'm hungry too when I miss a meal. But we'll have a
    big breakfast."

- Jeanne is tired in the morning because she stayed up too
  late:
  ANGRY WORDS: "I told you you'd be tired if you didn't
    go to bed on time. Now you're going to suffer all day
    at school."
  EMPATHETIC WORDS: "Oh, you're tired, huh? I feel the
    same way at work when I don't get my sleep. But
    have the best day you can, under the circumstances."

- Ray gets low grades on his report card:
  ANGRY WORDS: "You don't do your homework, and
    now you come home with lousy grades. That ought
    to teach you a lesson."
  EMPATHETIC WORDS: "Oh, how awful. During my
    school years, I got some poor grades when I didn't
    apply myself. But there's always next semester."

When no consequences occur naturally, the imposed consequences must (1) be enforceable, (2) fit the "crime," and (3) be laid down firmly in love. Sometimes these imposed consequences look conspicuously like punishments. But when imposed without anger and threats, and when presented to our children in a way that the connection between their misbehavior and the consequences is made plain, they are quite effective.

Two grade schoolers, Sally and Sue, are riding to the shopping center in the back seat of the family car. After they bicker, punch, and push, their mom draws the obligatory imaginary line down the middle of the back seat to keep them out of each others' hair. Then the screams from one or the other, "Mom, Sally's on my side!" or "Mom, Sue punched me!" And all of this happens even before the "Fasten Seat Belts" light has gone off on the dashboard.

Mom has had enough of it. The next time they were to go shopping, Mom said, "The last time we went to the shopping center, there was a lot of fighting in the back seat. It invaded my ears and made it so I couldn't concentrate on the road. I've decided to take a quiet drive to the stores today.

"I've arranged for a baby-sitter to stay with you. But don't worry about paying her right this minute. You can pay me on Saturday, or we can take it out of your allowance. But you don't need to decide about that right away. You can tell me later how you want to handle that."

This imposed consequence is enforceable. And because the time and place — going to the shopping center, riding in the car — both correspond to the previous problem experience, the consequence fits the "crime." The message is also laid down with thinking words.

When Billy comes home late from playing at a neighbor boy's house, a suitable consequence would be imposed the next time he asks to go to the neighbor boy's house by saying, "Remember how you were late coming home last time? I'm not up to worrying about that today, so you may stay home this time and play by yourself or watch television. We'll talk about it again the next time you want to go over there." The consequence is thus tied in Billy's mind to returning on time from the neighbor boy's house.

However, good consequences don't always pop right

into our brains. Even professionals in the field can't always think up immediate consequences.

If no consequence comes to mind, it is much better to take our time and think of an appropriate consequence than to blurt something out in haste or anger. We are no less effective as parents when we take a little time to think through consequences. Much-needed time for thinking can be bought with the following words:

- ◆ "I'm not sure what to do about this right now. But I'll let you know."
- ◆ "You know I've never been the parent of a five-year-old boy before. So I'll have to give this some thought. But I'll get back to you on it."
- ◆ "I'm not sure how to react to that. I'll have to give it some thought."

Giving ourselves time to consider consequences helps our kids, too. They have time to agonize over the possible consequences — and that is quality thinking time.

IT'S THE EMPATHY THAT COUNTS

You have probably noticed that love-and-logic parents react quite differently than other parents do when kids make mistakes. We don't get angry, we don't riddle them with I-told-you-so's, and we don't sit them down and lecture them about their errors.

If we get angry, we strip the consequences of their power. We insert ourselves into the process and impede the logic of the consequences from doing their thing. The child's anger is directed toward us and not toward the lesson the consequences teach.

Also, when we sit kids down and explain to them — even in the nicest terms — what they did wrong and why it didn't work out, we deflect their thinking from their own consequences to us. We only retard the power of the consequences when we do that.

The thing that drives the lesson down into our children's hearts after they make a mistake is our *empathy* and *sadness*. We put the relationship between us and our children foremost in our minds. Our love for them reigns supreme. We have been building their self-concept from infancy, telling them they are loved, skillful, and capable. And a foul-up, regardless of how serious on their part, doesn't change anything. They must know that, and be told that message continually.

LOVE-AND-LOGIC TIP 23
Messages that Lock in Empathy
Empathy with the consequences is so crucial to love-and-logic parenting. Yet when our kids mess up, we are often overcome with anger and want to punish them.

Before getting angry or sucked into the child's problem, try using one of the following statements:

- "What a bummer."
- "Really? I know you, and I'm sure you'll come up with something."
- "That's terrible. How are you going to handle it?"
- "Oh no, I'm glad that's not my paper (report card, grade, late assignment, specific problem, etc.). You must feel awful. What can you do?"
- "Hm-m-m, that's really an interesting way of looking at it. Let me know how that turns out."
- "Wow, what a mess. Let me know what you come up with."

When we make these types of comments we don't put ourselves up against our kids. We put ourselves squarely on their side, and on the side of their learning from their mistakes.

So, when they make a mistake, we really ache for them—we know what it's like. And we tell them this in all seriousness. When our kids blow it and suffer the consequences, it is crucial that we express our sadness to them.

Jane was well on her way to becoming a love-and-logic parent. She strove to give away the control she didn't need, and she always made sure Karla, her sixth-grade daughter, had to do more thinking than Jane did.

When Karla came home from school one day with a D on her spelling test, Jane's parenting philosophy was put to a more rigorous test—providing empathy with the consequences.

Jane kept hearing a voice in her head that said, "This could be a great opportunity. Don't blow it by reminding her." And Jane didn't reprimand her daughter. She also knew the school had provided the consequence, so she didn't say anything about that either.

Jane did exactly what she knew was right. She felt sorry for her daughter. She balanced the consequences with an equal amount of empathy. She said, "Oh, it must really be embarrassing to get a D. I bet it's hard to face your teacher when you haven't done your studying. I bet you feel awful."

Karla got very quiet and was thinking about what she had done. Then Jane thought of a love-and-logic principle: *When you run out of things to say, transfer the problem to the youngster by asking a question.* So Jane said, "What are you going to do, Karla?"

Karla, with a downcast face, meekly replied, "I don't know what I'm going to do."

So far so good. Jane had the control she needed, and Karla, with all her thinking, was owning the problem and devising solutions. But then Jane slipped up and said, "Since you refuse to study, you're not going to the party on Friday."

"What do you mean I'm not going to the party!" Karla yelled. "It's not my fault I got a D. You should see the words that teacher gives. She never gives us time to study, and she never helps me when I raise my hand, and . . . and . . . it's just not fair!"

Allowing consequences while showing empathy is one of the toughest parts of love-and-logic parenting. Anger is such an appealing emotion—especially when we use it on our children. Punishment makes us feel so powerful. It makes us think we're in control. Anger and punishment, put in concert with each other, provide a deadly duo of counter-productive parenting.

The entire lesson Karla was learning was demolished by Jane's anger and punishment. For the consequences to have any benefit, we must commiserate *with* our kids, not yell *at* them. They have nobody to be angry with but themselves when we show sadness. Because of anger and punishment, Karla had Jane and her teacher to blame.

We are constantly giving messages to our kids, but the overriding message of all messages must be one telling them that they're okay. They may be having a hard time with their lives. They may have made a mistake and will have to live with the consequences, but we're in their corner, we love them just the same. Empathy with the consequences shows them that kind of love. It allows the logic of the consequences to do the teaching.

8

LIGHTS, CAMERA, PARENTING

❖

I have taught you the way of wisdom;
I have led you in the paths
of uprightness.
When you walk, your step will
not be hampered;
and if you run, you will not stumble.
PROVERBS 4:11-12

A fifty-year-old man approached a musician and asked, "Can you teach me to play the trombone so I can play in the town civic band and in parades and other things?"

"Sure," the musician said.

"How long will it take?" the aspiring trombonist asked.

"Well," the musician said, "I could teach almost anybody to play anything he wanted to play in five years' time."

"Five years!" the would-be student said. "I'll be fifty-five years old by then!"

"Yes, you will," the musician returned. "And how old will you be in five years if you don't learn how to play the trombone?"

101

PRACTICE, PRACTICE, PRACTICE

The parenting with love and logic ideas may seem over-whelming to neophyte parents, or to parents frustrated with disciplining their children under different philosophies.

There's much to remember — self-concept, thinking words, separation of problems, choices, empathy with the consequences. It's enough to exasperate anyone unschooled in the love-and-logic style, if they were to try to apply it all at once.

Love-and-logic parenting is like dieting. Dieters do not say, "I'm going to become thin today," and presto, become thin. Likewise, parents don't say, "These kids of mine are going to shape up for good *right now*."

So, if love-and-logic is brand-new to you, implement it a little at a time. Pick one thing that bothers you about your child's behavior — one thing that you think you would have good success of correcting with love-and-logic prin-ciples — and then work on it. But don't do it right away. Rehearse it first. Figure out how your child might react and prepare yourself to meet that reaction. Once you've succeeded in one small area, pick another area and work on it, then another, and so on.

This technique is called *mental rehearsal*. The following five-point guideline will help you implement love and logic:

1. Pick the situation and what you want the child to do.
2. Picture yourself standing tall, looking directly into the child's eyes and having a perfect right to expect what you are about to request. Check yourself in a mirror.
3. Imagine the sound of your voice.
4. Try it out on friends and get their opinions.
5. Rehearse this until you hear yourself saying, "Kid, make my day. Let me strut my new stuff!"

The time to actually implement the strategy should be when you have the time, the energy, and enough back-up support for your actions. Kids will test you, they will get angry, they will try anything to make you revert to your old ways—even to the point of saying, "Mom, I liked you better the old way." But hold firm. Once you encounter resistance, you'll know it's working.

It usually takes one month of love-and-logic parenting to undo one year of tacky parenting. So, if your child is twelve years old, give yourself twelve months to help him or her learn responsible thinking.

Don't worry about the kids. They'll be happy to oblige you with practice opportunities. They have had years of experience in getting to parents, and they know a good thing when they see it. If they can control you by hitting your anger or sympathy or guilt button, they'll come rushing back to it whenever they feel the need for control.

You will find, as you implement love-and-logic parenting, that you will grow as much as your children do. With every success you experience, your self-concept will develop as much as theirs does.

It's never too late to use love and logic. Even if our kids are in their teens and have never been exposed to love-and-logic discipline, they—and we—can benefit from putting it to use. The important thing is to build a relationship with our kids that will last a lifetime—long past the end of the teenage years. And it is never too late to work on that.

Our children are our most precious resource. They come to us with one request: "During our short eighteen years with you, please teach us the truth about life and prepare us to be responsible adults when we leave home and enter the real world."

In the course of those eighteen years, we'll be faced with many challenges in parenting our kids. Our love will be on the line every time they have a problem. That love has the potential to be either ally or enemy—to either help our children learn what they need to know or prevent them from growing to be responsible adults.

Let's grant our kids' request. Let's love them enough to allow them to learn the necessary and crucial skill of responsible thinking and living.

PART II

*Love-and-Logic
Parenting Pearls*

How to Use
Love-and-Logic Pearls

Knowing some concepts on parenting is a good beginning; they offer a foundation on which to build a system of discipline. But putting those ideas into practical use puts us on ground decidedly more treacherous.

How do we handle children who pull a Mount Saint Helens' eruption whenever they don't win a struggle of wills? What about those little shavers who meet even our kindest inquiry with the words "Get out of my face, sucker"? How about the children who won't go to bed on time, or won't get up, or won't do chores, or homework, or feed the pets, or whatever?

We don't want philosophy. *We want answers!* How do separation of problems, thinking words, choices, and empathy with the consequences play themselves out in real, practical, get-down parenting?

The second half of this book, consisting of forty-one love-and-logic pearls, offers practical advice for handling some of the more common disciplinary problems a parent will meet during a child's first twelve years. In these pearls, we have explored and discussed individual topics and given sound, practical advice on how to deal with them. Many of the pearls also contain a sample dialogue that shows how to discuss the issue with the child.

But, reader beware: Do not try these pearls until you've read the first half of the book.

Pearl 1

❖

ALLOWANCES/MONEY

There comes a time in the life of every child when financial responsibility pokes its foreboding snout through the tent flap of his or her world. We call it an allowance. It usually begins when a child is five or six years old.

We give children allowances because we want to teach them money management. Kids who have to struggle with money not only become more fiscally responsible, they also become more responsible in all areas of life. In fact, it has been found that kids with good money-management skills tend to manage their jobs at school better, too.

Several helpful rules on allowances will help our kids make the most of this terrific learning experience.

Rule 1: Children do not earn their allowances. That means we do not pay them to do their chores. Being paid for chores robs them of the dignity of holding up their fair share of the family workload. The only time we'd pay them for chores is when they do our chores, that is, if we don't want to do them.

Rule 2: Provide the allowance at the same time every week. This can be done with pay envelopes. Place the cash, plus a small invoice indicating the breakdown of the funds—for example, for a child in first grade, "$1 allowance, $6 lunch money"–inside an envelope with the child's name on it. Sign the invoice, "Because we love you. Spend it wisely and make it last." The child must then tend to the envelope.

Rule 3: Never insist that children save the allowance. They can't learn to handle money if they stash their allowance in a shoe box at the back of their closet, saving it for when they get big. Kids must go through their own economic depression–wasting money, then not having any when they need it–to learn about money. In general, people–and kids, too–learn best to save only after they've learned how to be broke.

Rule 4: As long as they're not engaged in illegal activity, allow children to spend, save, or waste the money any way they see fit. They can use it to hire others to do their chores. They can even hire a baby-sitter if they don't want to go somewhere with the family.

But there's a catch: When it's gone, it's gone. No more allowance until the next week's envelope.

My (Jim's) son Charlie learned a powerful lesson in money management the very first week he got on the allowance payroll. Our family visited a carnival, and the midway barkers had their way with the boy. He came home flat broke.

"Dad, what am I going to do for lunch?" Charlie said when reality struck him on Monday morning.

"Go over to your pay envelope and get your lunch money out," I replied.

"But it's all gone," Charlie said.

"Oh, no, that's really too bad. What are you going to do?" I said.

"I don't know," Charlie said. "Can I get some food out of the refrigerator and make a lunch?"

"Sure, if you can afford to pay for it," I said. "Mom and I have already paid for lunches once, and we don't want to pay for them again."

It was a tough week for Charlie. But surviving for five days on two meals a day (we made sure they were good ones) taught him a big lesson in money management.

There will be times, however, when kids are more persistent—and more psychologically devious—than Charlie. When they blow their bankroll early and shuffle up to us begging for more money before the appointed allowance time, we must become as tight as a Depression-era banker. There will be more money, sure—on allowance day. Even when our kids push the powerful guilt button, we must make sure nothing moves out of our pockets.

Observe how this dad handles daughter Steffi's mid-week crisis:

STEFFI: "Dad, I need more allowance."

DAD: "Yeah, that's kind of how it is for me. I always need more money in my paycheck than I get. Have you got any ideas about what you're going to do?"

STEFFI: "Yeah. I'm asking you. Dad, could you give me more allowance?"

DAD: "Well, I'll be happy to give you your allowance on Saturday. But for now, maybe you'll consider bidding on someone else's chores around the house so you can earn some money that way."

STEFFI: "But I need it now!"

DAD: "Boy, I bet you do. But don't worry, you'll get more on Saturday."

STEFFI: "That's not fair!"

DAD: "That could be true, and there will be more on Saturday."

STEFFI: "My friends don't have this problem because their parents love them and give them more money."

DAD: "I bet that's true too, *and* there will be more on Saturday."

If Steffi keeps it up, Dad could put a finishing touch to the discussion by saying, "If I kept carrying on like that to my boss, how do you suppose he'd feel about my job? He'd feel like paying me less, wouldn't he? So, do your best to solve this, Steffi. We'll see you later."

Pearl 2

❖

Anger: When It's Appropriate

As a general rule, the decision on whether or not to use anger in our dealings with our children hinges on the issue of separation of problems. Kids' problems should always be met with our empathy. They got themselves into the mess. The gain in their responsibility can be won only if we commiserate with them, not if we shout at them when they're working it out.

If our kids mistakes only hurt them and not us — if they trip and fall, or throw their fists and come home with a black eye, or fail half-a-dozen classes at school — then our anger makes the problem worse.

It's a lot like the hot-rodding husband who hugs bumpers in the fast lane and pushes the needle into the red zone. If his wife screams, "Honey, stop it! You're doing seventy-five!" it only makes him angry. Because he's the one driving, he thinks that the speed is his concern, and he resents interference from his wife.

But if the wife says, "Honey, I don't want to die," she's bringing her own welfare into the equation. Her anger is understandable and effective. He can take *that*.

When our kids do something that affects us directly — lose our tools, leave their trikes in the driveway, fail to put our things away after using them—then it's okay for us to get a bit huffy. They will recognize that we're angry because their misbehavior has affected us.

Little Barb, in her eagerness to cut out paper dolls, broke her mom's scissors. Mom, realizing that anger was entirely appropriate, said, "Barb, I'm so angry I can't see straight. Now I can't even use my own scissors. I expect you to do something to make this right. Be prepared to tell me before you go to bed tonight what you are going to do." Notice that Mom did not demean the child with her anger; she didn't tell Barb how stupid and irresponsible she was. Instead, she focused on how Barb's action affected her and the need for a solution.

Anger is also generally appropriate if we've made a rational decision to use it. Occasionally, kids need to be read a sixty-second riot act. They need a show of anger. We can ponder these options: "Do I want to isolate my child? Or do I want to talk it over with him or her and do some problem solving? Or do I think this child needs a sixty-second rant and a hug afterward, with me saying, 'The reason I'm so angry, dear, is because you're the type of kid who could handle the situation so much better.'"

The decision to use anger must be dispassionate, not a flying-off-the-handle, finger-poking-the-chest bawl out. Generally speaking, anger should be used only when our children's behavior directly affects us.

One note of caution: We should not use anger so often that it becomes an expected emotion. All of us, including our kids, love emotion. Once kids get used to a particular emotion—be it shame, anger, guilt, or love—that expected emotion becomes the emotion of choice.

Pearl 3

❖

BEDTIME

"Time for bed, sweetie." You say it every night. And every night you have to jump through all sorts of hoops before you get any action.

It's always something: "After this program ends." "Can I have something to eat first?" "Read me a story." "But I'm not tired." "There are monsters in my room." When it comes to finding reasons for not crawling under the covers, every kid is an Einstein.

The fact is, *you cannot make children go to sleep.* Their eyes will close and the dreams will descend on them when their body clocks tell them to. All the parental orders in the world can't make it happen.

Different kids require different amounts of sleep. Recent research has shown that brighter children, particularly gifted children, may not need as much sleep as others. Too bad. They are bright enough that they may be more of a problem when they're awake. In reality, God has determined how much sleep kids need — and it varies from child to child.

The sad thing with many parents is that they put their children to bed simply to get them out of their hair in the evening. These parents say, "Mommy and Daddy are tired, so it's time for you kids to go to bed." Ideally, the children should be able to be up *and* out of their parents' hair—at the same time.

Instead of saying, "This is how much sleep you need every night," the love-and-logic parent says, "This is how much you have an *opportunity* to sleep at night because you're in your room."

That opportunity can begin at 7:30 or 8:30 or some other time. Allow the child and your need for privacy to determine the time. This takes the heat out of the bedtime battle. In fact, it makes it no battle at all.

Bedtime, like many other control issues, can be defused by giving up control. Parents tend to underestimate children's need for just a tiny bit of control. So, when they see their kids going for all the control, they think that's what the children really want. In reality, all they want is a little control—not the whole enchilada.

So give it up. Ask your children if they'd rather be in their room quietly with their door open or with it closed, with their room light on or off, with their night light on or off, with the radio on softly or off. Ask your kids if they'd like to hear a bedtime story first or not. Don't hold all the cards; cut them in on the action, too.

A discussion of the bedtime issue with your child might sound like this:

> PARENT: "How much sleep do you think you need at night?"
> CHILD: "Not very much. I like to be up at night."
> PARENT: "Is that right? I can understand that. But you know, I'm the type of person who needs eight hours of sleep and about two hours of 'alone' time every night. So that's ten hours when we won't be together."
> CHILD: "Oh. Uh-huh."
> PARENT: "Would you rather my 'alone' time start at

8:00, or at 8:30? Now, when I start my alone time
that means you need to be in your room. You
can read if you want, or you can go to sleep. So,
which time would you prefer?"
CHILD: "I don't know."
PARENT: "Well, if you don't know, then I'll probably
pick a time."
CHILD: "Okay, 8:30. Can I have my light on?"
PARENT: "Sure."
CHILD: "Can I play music?"
PARENT: "Yes, as long as I can't hear it."
CHILD: "Do I have to be in bed?"
PARENT: "Nope."
CHILD: "Can I sleep on the floor?"
PARENT: "No problem."

Many of us won't grant this sort of control for fear
of the consequences. We're afraid that little Gary—up till
1:00 a.m., rocking with his radio and sorting his baseball
cards—is going to be one obnoxious little dude in the
morning.

We're right, of course. But that doesn't mean Gary has
to be an obnoxious dude around us. It's the obnoxiousness
we consequence, not the number of hours he sleeps. Don't
think, "Now, he's obnoxious, therefore, I've got to make him
sleep more." Do think, "He's obnoxious, therefore, I can provide him with a super learning experience." Then say to the
child, "You need to spend more time in the recreation room
(or in his room, or anywhere, as long as it's away from you)
because you're cranky."

The child will probably say, "Well, I didn't get enough
sleep last night."

And your reply? "Good thinking." The lesson will hit
home.

Pearl 4

❖

BOSSINESS

Is it any wonder that bossy parents often have bossy kids? Parents who order their children around like boot-camp recruits end up with kids who want to be drill sergeants. It makes perfect sense.

Little children love to act big. If they see the big people in their lives bossing, they'll boss, too. So, the first place to look for fault with bossy kids is ourselves. If we command out kids to jump and expect them to say, "How high?" our kids will be mirror images of us in their dealings with their playmates.

However, it's not always the parents who are at fault. Even non-bossy moms and dads have bossy kids on occasion. Oftentimes these children are simply addicted to having their own way, and bossing others is one way to accomplish that goal.

Occasionally these control-conscious children will even turn their demanding mouths on us. *That* we won't tolerate. One way to handle this is to have a good one-liner or two ready for immediate use.

When the bossy bit happens, our first response is a genuine extended smile at the child. This unexpected turn of events gives him or her time to think, to wonder what in the world is going on. Then, quietly, we say something like, "Nice try, Tammy. Nice try. What do you think happens in this family when people get really bossy? Does it help or not? But please don't answer that now. Just give it some thought." Then we walk off.

We deal with bossy children without injecting any emotion into the atmosphere. We also don't lay into them with "Don't you *dare* order me around!" Their behavior is dealt with rationally and forthrightly.

When our children boss other kids around, however, then we become counselors. After all, now it's one of their problems, not ours.

> MOM: "Tammy, I notice that you're kind of bossy with those other kids. Do you ever worry that this might make them not like you? They wouldn't be your friends anymore then."
>
> TAMMY: "Aw, they'd still be my friends."
>
> MOM: "I just wonder how it'll work out. Of course, you might be one of those rare people who can boss others around and still make them be friends. What do you think? Have you figured out any ways you can boss them around and still keep them as friends?"
>
> TAMMY: "I don't know."
>
> MOM: "Well, I'll be interested to watch and see how it goes. I hope it works out for you."

Chances are that somewhere along the line it won't work out. The real world will drive the lesson home — rudeness equals losing friends and making enemies. Other kids happily provide learning experiences for bossy kids like Tammy.

Then, when Tammy returns to Mom's side with her problem, Mom can express the sadness of a true friend:

MOM: "Oh, so that really didn't work out, huh,
    Tammy?"
TAMMY: "No."
MOM: "That's really sad. What do you suppose you'll
    do to get your friends back?"
TAMMY: "I don't know."
MOM: "I sure hope that works out for you. If you
    ever decide you want me to give you some ideas
    about working with other kids so that they don't
    feel bossed around, let me know. I'll be glad to
    talk with you about it."

Telling our kids not to be so bossy only bosses them and makes them mad at us—and the bossiness will continue. But putting the burden of the problem on their shoulders, and always being nearby with a word of advice if it's asked for, will push them toward solution.

Pearl 5

---❖---

CAR: BACK-SEAT BATTLES

It starts benignly. Kent trespasses onto Molly's "space" in the back seat of the family car. And Molly yells, "Mom, Kent's on my side."

Then Molly socks him on the arm. "Keep your filthy paws on your own side, Kent," she demands. Kent retreats to his arm rest to regroup, for Molly is marginally larger than he and packs a meaner right jab. But the provocateur in Kent cannot be subdued. Carefully, he inches his right hand toward the middle of the seat. First his forefinger, then the rest of his fingers, then his whole hand moves into his sister's space.

"Mom!" Molly yells. "Make him stop!" Then she attacks: fists, screams, hair-pulling — World War III in the back seat.

There is something about the back seat of a moving car that excites kids. Call it cabin fever. Call it claustrophobia. Call it seizing the moment when parents are otherwise occupied. But put two or more of them in the same car together, and kids turn into a cross between guerilla warriors and stool pigeons. They fight, they argue, they hassle each other, and they hassle us.

So we say, "You guys shut up back there." While this

may provide temporary relief, it usually fails to have lasting effect. In fact, it may last only a few blocks, at which point we are forced to say something even stronger.

The back-seat problem is one we can and should nip in the bud. If we handle the problem when it's not really serious, it will never become serious. But we must choose the time wisely: when we aren't in a hurry to get anywhere, and when it doesn't matter how long we take to get our message across. Our message is, put simply: We're not going to tolerate back-seat bickering, and if it continues, *something* is going to happen.

Consider the following for kids who are in grade school: Arnold was ready for anything his back-seat warriors could hit him with one morning. He had rehearsed his lines and even brought a paperback with him to kill the time he expected to be wasting on the trip.

Right on schedule, his kids started going at each other in the back seat. Arnold stopped the car, turned very calmly around, and said, "You know, guys, I think the hard thing about being cooped up in a tiny car like this is that the oxygen level in your blood gets low, then you get irritated and fight. But if you can get out of the car and replenish it, things always get better. Why don't you guys get out of the car and work your problem out, and replenish your oxygen level at the same time? I'll just drive ahead and wait for you."

As protection for his kids, Arnold added, "Now, if you don't walk too close to the cars going down the street, and if you stay on the sidewalk, I'm sure you'll be safe and you won't get hit."

Then he drove up the street several blocks to a place where his kids could see him, parked the car, and read his book. He could see them jawing at each other and getting on each other's case as they walked. But as they neared the car, they got better and better. By the time they got to the car, they were calm.

As one child reached for the door handle and started

to open the door, the other jumped in front and the war resumed. So Arnold pulled up another few blocks and parked there to read his book. When his kids got there, they were in pretty good shape.

Now, whenever he drives down the road and his kids start to get rowdy, he simply says, "Hey, guys, are you needing to replenish the oxygen supply?" and his kids pipe down right quick.

Here's another idea for handling back-seat bickering: Margaret called her best friend one evening to explain her problem and ask for a favor: "Can you follow my car on Saturday morning at 11:30? Just do a little FBI surveillance for me, okay? Stay a few car lengths back. When we get to Third and Main, I'm sure I'm going to be throwing a couple of kids out of the car. I've always been afraid of doing this before because the kids might get kidnapped or something. But I could have the confidence to do it if you were watching them and making sure they were safe."

Next morning, true to form, by the time Margaret's car reached First and Main, the kids were screaming like little Morton Downey Jr.'s. Margaret said, "Guys, I can't drive with that noise. It hassles my mind."

The kids hit the volume knob. They *knew* Mom wasn't going to do anything—she never had before—and they felt safe no matter how loud they got.

Margaret gave them another chance to amend their ways. "Hey, guys," she yelled over the din, "I've got to tell you that I can't drive with that noise." But, to no avail.

So right at Third and Main, Margaret pulled the car over, went around to the other side of the car, and opened the kids' door. "We can't walk home," they said. "We'll be kidnapped."

But Margaret hung tough. This was, after all, what her rehearsal had been for. She said, "Keep your eyes down. Don't look up, and maybe nobody will bother you. I'll see you at home." And she took off.

Later her friend told her, "You didn't need me. You should have seen those kids walking home. They looked so somber. They never did look up."

For some reason, Margaret's kids listen to her now.

This technique works for smaller children as well (e.g., preschoolers). However, be reasonable about the distance between you and the child—three-fourths of a block is far enough. Make sure that you or someone else can watch the entire episode.

One final back-seat battle example: Mom and Dad were driving on a busy highway far from home. Putting misbehaving kids out of the car was out of the question, so the kids seized the moment.

Dad pulled the car off the road and onto the shoulder as far as possible. Mom and Dad got out of the car and, without a word, walked up on a little knoll and sat down. They talked and pointed at things and seemed to be enjoying themselves. (Another possibility would have been for the lucky couple to stop at an ice cream shop.)

Soon, from the car, they heard things like, "Shut up, or they're never going to come back here," and "You'd better be quiet." When all was quiet on the back-seat front, the parents got back in and drove off.

Thirty minutes later the back-seat clatter started again, but as Dad steered the car toward the right shoulder, this refrain came pouring over the headrests: "Shut up! Here they go again."

If we can pull one of these tactics when there is no hurry to get anywhere, then when we are in a hurry, one little word directed toward the back seat will get results.

Pearl 6

❖

CHORES

Nothing warms the heart like the sight of our children industriously flitting about the house completing their chores. We see them assuming a sense of responsibility and belonging, and we are right proud. Plus, there's work being done, progress being made, our property being cared for. Oh, happy, happy!

Come now, this isn't utopia. More commonly, chores are dreaded—by parents and youngsters alike. The fact is, hands don't shoot up in giddy excitement when we ask, "Who wants to do the dishes?" Happy feet don't scurry for the broom and hose when we say, "Okay, who wants to clean the garage today?" But if handled properly, we *can* take the hassle out of chores. And we start when our kids are small.

When they are little, kids enjoy doing things with their parents. We say "doing things *with*" instead of "helping" because, face it, what they do is not real help. They just naturally like to copy us. They like to stir around in the water as mom does dishes. They like to push around their little lawn mowers when dad cuts the grass. When it snows, they cry rivers if we don't buy them little plastic shovels so they can "help" scoop the walks. (Too bad they don't do that when they're twelve!)

The secret to instilling a good attitude in our kids about chores (hang on, this may sound like bad news) is that *we* must have fun while doing them. If we make it drudgery, then our little ones will think, "If that is what doing chores is like, count me out." Getting them to do anything around the house for the next twelve to fourteen years will resemble arms negotiations.

So, during the toddler years, we should get the idea across that work is fun. Wise parents will say things like,

- "Hey, do I ever like getting my jobs done around the house. It's fun for me!"
- "Wow, do I ever enjoy doing things with you!"
- "We sure have fun together!"

As kids reach an age when they can be held responsible—kindergarten or first grade—they should be given some very elementary tasks around the house, like cleaning up messes they make, helping clean their rooms, and making their beds (although not up to hospital standards).

By third grade and throughout the rest of grade school, they're ready to periodically wash dishes, vacuum the family room, sweep out the garage, take out the trash, wipe out the refrigerator, and help clean dirty windows and the car (inside and out).

However, there will be static. Kids have nimble minds. They will find excuses for not doing their chores, or they'll argue about who does what, or they'll complain about when they have to do them.

Love-and-logic parents negotiate with their children on chores. They tack a list of all chores onto a prominent place in the kitchen, then ask their kids to read it and decide which chores they would most like to do. A day or two later the whole family sits down to divvy them up. Rather than the parents deciding who does what, allow the kids themselves that control. If the chores are distributed unfairly, for whatever reason, the "unfaired upon" kid will quickly smell a con job and request renegotiation.

My (Foster's) kids once sat down to palaver over chores. What seemed to be a very inequitable arrangement was agreed to between Jerry, age fifteen, and Melinda, age eleven. The chores were: feeding the dog and doing dishes. The dog food was in the basement, and because Melinda was afraid of the dark, she opted for doing dishes every day instead of testing the unseen terrors of the basement. It didn't take long, however, for Melinda to see the unfair division of labor—and to overcome her fear of the dark. A renegotiation of jobs came about. Kids will work out chore problems between them when they're given some control.

A bigger problem is getting the chores done on your time schedule. Wise parents establish a time frame with phrases like, "by the next time you eat" or "by the time I take you to your soccer game (swimming lesson, or friend's house)." That way the child always knows the ground rules.

If chores are resisted a conversation may go something like this:

> PARENT: "Now, is it reasonable for me to assume that you will do the dishes by the end of the day?"
> CHILD: "Yeah, I guess I can do them by then."
> PARENT: "Well, that would be great. Now, let me ask you: When does the day end?"
> CHILD: "I go to bed about 9:30."
> PARENT: "That's a good point. But when exactly does the day end?"
> CHILD: "Well, midnight?"
> PARENT: "That's right. The thing is, though, if you don't get it done today, that means you'll have to get it done tomorrow. Now, when does tomorrow start?"
> CHILD: "That'd be at 12:01."
> PARENT: "There you go. So if not today—and I

would like it done today—that means you'll have to do it when?"

CHILD: "You mean you're going to get me up at 12:01 to do it?"

PARENT: "You got it, honey."

CHILD: "You can't do that!"

PARENT: "Well, it'll be exciting to find out anyhow, won't it?"

One sort of parent who ends up with resistant kids is the "Oh, by the way" parent. The simple sight of a child sitting in a chair reading sends these parents into deep flights of remembering. They remember all the jobs around the house that haven't been done—jobs that haven't even been assigned.

The "Oh, by the way" parents say things like, "Oh, by the way, can you pick up the trash in the yard?" or "Oh, by the way, can you polish the grillwork on the car?"

My (Foster's) mom pulled this on me when I was young, and I ended up doing my reading in the furnace room.

Pearl 7

❖

CHURCH: WHEN KIDS DON'T WANT TO GO

Responsible parents want to bring their children up with established spiritual values. They want their kids to have faith, to understand the Christian message, to know God intimately. That means the family's involvement in their church and its activities.

Unfortunately, there comes a time in our children's lives when they don't want to go to church. They have to sit still for so long. They don't really understand what the guy up front is talking about. Their Sunday clothes make them feel like there's an army of ants loose in the linings.

A more important—and in many cases more ominous—reason for many kids' dislike of church is rebellion against parental values (see pearl 40, "Values: Passing Them on to Your Kids"). Children learn early in life that their parents can't get into their brains. We can't make them think what we think or believe what we believe. When we try, we invite their disobedience; the kids see us usurping control, and they want to grab some of it back.

This is another area of parenting where proper modeling is vital. If from our children's infancy on, we have spoken positively about going to church—oftentimes to each other but within earshot of the children—we will have encouraged

129

our kids to like going to church, without coercion.

We want to make genuine well-placed statements like, "I'm sure glad I have my church. I enjoy my friends and always get such needed encouragement while I'm there," or "I always feel a lot better when I go to church. It really helps me keep my values in place." Positive statements can set the bug in our kids' ears and lessen their inclination to rebel.

At some point, however, our kids may dig in their heels and make a stand. It is often valuable to attempt to uncover the reasons for their displeasure with church. Maybe they hate their Sunday school teacher. Or they've had the baby Moses story for the past six years running and are bored stiff. Or there are few kids their age. It could be any number of things. Talking it out with our kids may help them see the value of the Sunday morning time with God.

And, of course, there are always ways to make children go to church—tactics we don't advise. When we do this, we do not allow them to appreciate and value the experience of their own volition. We can exert our power and feel in control, or we can look for a creative long-term solution.

The important thing to remember is that parental demands will probably come to fruition in rebellion. Kids will fight parents who insist that "you believe what I believe."

But have faith. Disliking church is most likely a stage. As little kids, they love Sunday school. Then comes the phase when they don't want to go. However, if we haven't made church attendance *the* spiritual issue during the early years—presenting a good role model instead—our kids will almost always see value in going to church as they get older.

Pearl 8

◆

CRISIS SITUATIONS

Drug use. Kids who run away from home. Debilitating injury. Suicide. A death in the family. A crippling disease.

When a crisis hits our lives or the lives of our children, it can send us reeling. Guilt, worry, anxiety, anger, and inconsolable grief are some of the emotions that can stagger us.

One of the most damaging ideas we carry into a crisis situation is that something must be done *right now*. This is seldom true. The character denoting crisis in the Chinese language is a combination of the symbols for danger and opportunity. We see the danger all too well, but we often miss the opportunity.

The following four thoughts may help us deal with a crisis.

First, crises, by their very nature, are generally temporary. There are usually better times ahead. Knowing this, we can guard against over involvement.

Second, almost no crisis must be dealt with immediately. We usually have time to pray and to think and act rationally, and to seek advice from others who have had a similar experience or who are professionally capable of dealing with it.

Also, many of what we perceive to be crises are not

crises at all. The problem may have been going on for months or even years, and only becomes a crisis when we find out about it. So we need to adopt the proper mind-set. If we suddenly discover our child has been taking drugs, this is a serious happening, true. But it's not necessarily a crisis. We have time to take care of it properly.

We may even want to consider doing nothing about the crisis. Granted, in many cases this is not a good solution. But we should still consider the option. Just doing *something* is not the answer. Doing the right thing is.

After writing all the options down—from the most active response to the least—we should talk them over with someone we respect. A clear-thinking perspective is the key.

Third, to help us cope, we must always ask ourselves what the worst possible outcome of the crisis would be. Many times we find we are able to deal with that. Not to be flippant about it, but the worst possible outcome—death—is inevitable anyway and can be faced if we are ready to meet our Maker.

Finally, we always need to keep the monkey on the back of the person responsible for the problem. If our child is using drugs, that's still his or her problem, regardless of our agony.

In summary, when a crisis erupts, we should take a moment, pray, breathe deeply, relax, write down all possible options, talk them over with a person we respect, think about our ability to cope with the worst possible outcome, and keep the faith. After all, that's our best weapon.

Pearl 9

◆

DISCIPLINE IN PUBLIC — STRATEGIC TRAINING SESSION

Kids are born smart. Even before they can speak intelligibly, they know when to apply the needle to us. More times than not, their bigger triumphs are in a store, a shopping center, a restaurant, and other public places.

You've been there. Put little Judy in the front of your shopping cart and she launches into her fire engine imitation. Take your eyes off little Jon for one second at church and before you know it he's chewing on Mrs. Smith's nylons three pews away. If you scold them, they let out a wail that makes Mick Jagger sound like a member of the Vienna Boys Choir.

As one mother put it, "Little Julie behaves just great when we happen to be going somewhere she wants to go, but just let it be a shopping trip for me and the kid goes wild. It always seems to happen in a public place where I just can't gain control of the situation. Everybody stares at us, and I'm so embarrassed that I could die."

Kids think their parents don't dare do anything to them because they're out in public. Parents think they don't dare consequence their kids with so many people looking on. The people watching wonder why in the world those parents don't do something about that obnoxious kid!

When you put it all together, it can get pretty hairy. And you wondered why parents of little kids like to shop alone?

But a public place is no different from the family living room. True, it doesn't lend itself to meaningful parent-child discussion, but that doesn't mean we forget love-and-logic principles. Children who misbehave in a public place must be disciplined. Otherwise, every trip to the store sets the stage for a disaster.

One technique for breaking this bad habit is called the "Strategic Training Session." It is somewhat involved and takes planning and cooperation from friends or family members. But done once, the lesson will take, and public kid attacks will be a thing of the past.

Laura tried it with her daughter Holly. She phoned her best friend one evening and said, "I've been having trouble with Holly when I go shopping, and I need your help. Would you station yourself at the pay phone outside this store tomorrow morning at 10:30? I have a feeling you're going to get a call." Laura then filled her friend in on the plan.

The next day Laura and Holly went shopping, and true to form, Holly became her usual obnoxious self even before the automatic doors of the store had closed behind them. In a quiet voice, Laura said, "Holly, would you rather behave or go sit in your room?"

Holly looked quizzically at her mom as if to say, "Get real, Mom. You'd take me home after you've come all the way down here to shop?" Then she ratcheted her attack up a notch.

The next thing Holly knew she was being led to a pay phone in the store where Laura dialed a number and said, "Shopping is not fun today. Please come."

Thirty seconds later, Holly's eyes grew as big as pie plates when her mom's friend strolled through the door, took Holly's hand, and said, "Let's go to your room. You can wait for your mom there."

Holly was escorted home and sent to her room. Laura was freed to make her rounds in unharried bliss. Holly was allowed out of her room when Laura returned. She was very happy to see her mom again, while Laura was friendly and pleasant because she had a great time shopping. Laura taught her little girl that, even in public, obnoxious behavior has consequences.

Strategic Training Sessions can be arranged with a spouse, or even an older sibling. It is not necessary to take the misbehaving child home, to the car is far enough—if the parents' co-conspirator can watch, undetected, from a distance.

There is absolutely no reason for our kids to get away with hellish behavior in public simply because we're with them. One, or at most two, Strategic Training Sessions can cure this problem.

Pearl 10

❖

DISCIPLINE 101
(BASIC GERMAN SHEPHERD) —
AGE ELEVEN TO EIGHTEEN MONTHS

Kids and dogs. Believe it or not, at age nine months children surpass the family dog in intelligence. In fact, when children are eleven to thirteen months old, they are old enough to learn the same things we teach our dog—that is, follow the commands "come, sit, go, no, stay." We call this "Basic German Shepherd."

Basic German Shepherd must be learned by the time the child is eighteen months old. It is the foundation of all discipline. If we can't make a two-year-old obey basic commands, the next sixteen years of that child's life and ours will be pure torture.

The key to teaching Basic German Shepherd is to control only what we can control. We can never make an infant stop crying, quit bothering us, stop sucking his or her thumb, or cut the whining. What we can and should control, though, is *where* he or she does all these things.

If our children ignore our firm "please stop" once, with no pleading or whining on our part, then they should be given the opportunity to act obnoxiously someplace else. And that place is in their room. They can act like jerks if they want to, as long as they're in their own room. But getting them there can be a problem.

The first step in moving our kids to their room is teaching them to sit and stay in the same room with us when they're obnoxious—sit them in a corner. It may be tough on our ears—they will probably be screaming bloody murder—but it is necessary. When our children start to get up, we should establish strong eye contact and say meaningfully (not loudly and certainly not with a scream), "I said 'stay.'" After our children develop this skill, the next step is to put them in a nearby room where we can keep an eye on them.

Later when the obnoxious behavior begins, we send them to cry in their own room. But remember, we are not sending them there to punish them. We are merely giving them the opportunity to pull themselves together. If they come out still angry and obnoxious, we send them back to stay an added five minutes for every year of their age.

We should *never* forget to show love to our kids. When their good mood returns, they need to be hugged and rocked for doing things right.

Once we have mastered this elementary discipline technique, we have a very long leg up on any subsequent parent-child encounters. Since so much of parenting with love and logic revolves around changing the location rather than the behavior, without Basic German Shepherd we are in big trouble.

Three common mistakes surface in the teaching of Basic German Shepherd. First, we can be too tough. Little kids are, at times, no fun. Aren't we all? If our parents were too strict or overly permissive, we might be tempted to overuse Basic German Shepherd. Remember, everyone has a right to be crabby and moody at times—even our kids. For example, if we've kept our young child up far past the normal bedtime and he or she is a total grump the next day, is it fair for us to sentence the child to solitary confinement? Understanding and common sense go a long way in parent-child relationships.

Second, we can be too lenient, putting up with too much before we issue the "go" command. Too much malarkey stretches our tolerance, and by the time we say "adios" to our child, we may be angry rather than effective.

Third, we may confuse anger with firmness. A firm person may be loud, or may even use a little physical pressure, but firm I-mean-business people don't yell and scream and are seldom frustrated with anger.

Some parents think eleven-to-sixteen-month-old children are too young to learn Basic German Shepherd (kids will use this to their advantage). However, most normal children's receptive language is developed well enough at that age to know exactly what we are saying and expecting. In fact, if young children are allowed to annoy their parents unmercifully, it almost always contributes to their poor self-image.

Pearl 11

---❖---

DISCIPLINE 201
(REMEDIAL GERMAN SHEPHERD)—
AGE FOUR TO SIX YEARS

This pearl is for those of us who have failed Basic German Shepherd. If our children are now between four and six years old and they still *no comprende* when we give one of the basic commands—come, sit, go, no, stay—we have a problem. After all, Basic German Shepherd is the foundation of all discipline. It lays the groundwork for our modeling, where we *demonstrate* to our children that happy people do not put up with hassles from one another. By age two, at the latest, children should have Basic German Shepherd down pat.

If somehow our children have slipped through the cracks of our disciplinary system and at age four to six don't have the basics, we may have to do some remedial work. The following nine rules apply to controlling, in a good way, an out-of-control kindergartner or first grader:

1. Avoid all physical tussles. For instance, small mothers should not try to wrangle big sons to their rooms.
2. Use orders sparingly. Never give a child an order you cannot make him or her follow.
3. Tell your child what you wish he or she would do

rather than giving an order.

4. Give a complete "I message": "I would appreciate your going to your room now, so I can feel better about you and me." ("I messages" tell your feelings and why you feel that way.)

5. Sometimes when a request is given, it is wise to thank the child in advance, anticipating compliance.

6. When the child is in a good mood, talk things over, exploring his or her feelings and laying down expectations for the future.

7. Use isolation and/or a change of location for behavior problems, rather than trying to stop the behavior.

8. Use corporal punishment very sparingly, if at all, and then only as outlined in pearl 31, "Spanking."

9. Be emotional when things are done right; be matter of fact, nonemotional, and consequential — using isolation — when things are done poorly or wrongly.

With these rules in mind, let's listen as Elaine attempts to send her five-year-old son Jesse to his room:

JESSE: "Mom, come here right now!"
ELAINE: (wonders what's going through his head)
JESSE: "Mom! I said, 'Come here'!"
ELAINE: "Hey, kiddo, I don't like it when you talk to me that way. I'd like you to scoot up to your room and give it some thought."
JESSE: "No! I'm not going!"
ELAINE: "Jesse, I would like you to go to your room."
JESSE: "No!"
ELAINE: "Jesse, I think you are making a poor choice."
JESSE: "You can't make me go."
ELAINE: "I don't want to make you. You are making

a poor choice. It would be wise for you to go to
your room now."
JESSE: "No!"
ELAINE: "Well, I'm disappointed. I wish you had
given it more careful thought."

Elaine failed, right? Wrong. She merely handled what
she could handle. She refrained from spanking—which is
usually effective only for children under the age of three.
She didn't carry the boy to his room. She also didn't issue
an order she couldn't enforce. All of her comments were
"I messages." Correct moves. But she didn't get results. So
later she enlisted the support of her husband, Dean. Elaine
talked the situation over with him when he returned home
from work, and then they engaged Jesse in the following
discussion at the dinner table:

DEAN: "How did the day go, honey?"
ELAINE: "Oh, pretty good. But Jesse had trouble
going to his room."
DEAN: (incredulously) "You're kidding?"
ELAINE: (sounding surprised herself) "No, it's a
fact, dear."
DEAN: "Well, do you think he needs practice,
honey?"
JESSE: "I don't need practice. I know how to do it."
DEAN: (with powerful firmness) "You know that
when your mother says move, you should move."
JESSE: "All right, all right."
DEAN: "How much practice does he need, honey?
A hundred trips?"
ELAINE: "No, I think probably twenty from here
to his room will do. We don't want to give him
more practice than he needs. Jesse's a fairly
smart kid."
DEAN: "Okay, Jesse, you can finish your dinner

after you've made twenty trips to and from your
room. Start now! Fast!"

JESSE: "But . . . ."

DEAN: "How do I want you to go?"

JESSE: "Fast."

DEAN: "How do I want you to move?"

JESSE: "Fast!"

DEAN: "Thank you. Now move out."

JESSE: "Okay, I'm going. I'm going."

When Elaine was dealing with Jesse, notice that she
didn't cut herself down. She didn't say, "Wait until your
dad gets home." On the contrary, she stayed in charge the
whole time. Later she was even kind, cutting the practice to
twenty during the dinnertime training session.

As for Dean, he was extremely firm without losing his
self-control. He said what he meant and he meant what
he said. Most importantly, he backed his wife to the hilt.
He didn't allow Jesse to drive a wedge between Elaine
and him.

If the four-to-six-year-old still refuses to go to his or her
room when sent, more drastic measures are needed. Parents
may want to leave the child with a sitter (see pearl 28, "The
Room: Keeping the Kid in It"), or we may wish to use isolation, before trying the technique again. A well-planned swat
also may get the desired result. If the child still won't follow
the direction to go to his or her room after a few attempts,
professional help is needed.

Pearl 12

---❖---

Divorce and Visitation

When parents divorce each other, the casualty list includes more than the husband and wife. Kids suffer too. They may experience mood swings, defensiveness about being touched, reversion to elimination problems (younger children), hyperactivity (grade school children), back talk (teenagers), and general problems with school work, lack of interest, and laziness.

Luckily, such behavior is often part of a normal grieving process and can be alleviated by following these ten guidelines for divorced or divorcing parents.

Guideline one: Expect children to handle the divorce about as well as the adults handle it. If a divorce is marked by bitterness, lack of communication, and anger, the children will probably behave in much the same way as the parents.

Guideline two: Let the children know that the divorce is not their fault. As adults, we know children seldom cause divorces. Nevertheless, some children may think, "If I had been a better kid, my parents wouldn't be divorcing." A parent can say, "Michael, you know that some kids are friends and then decide they can't get along. Well, that's kind of what has happened with Dad and me. But we both still love *you*."

Guideline three: Be honest about feelings and observations. Parents need to tell their children, without details, how they feel about the ex-spouse and why. It is also helpful to give the other parent's point of view. While it is important to let children know our concerns, it is equally important to let them know that the ex-spouse continues to love them (if that is true). Bad-mouthing the ex-spouse backfires.

Guideline four: Understand children's misbehavior without excusing it. Encourage your children to express their feelings, but continue to give consequences for misbehavior. Parents must never tolerate disrespect.

Guideline five: Give children a support group. Children need someone outside the family to talk with — school counselors, teachers, peer groups, or friends of the family.

Guideline six: Post-divorce counseling for parents and children may help. When communication is poor and distrust rampant between the adults, counseling is almost always helpful, especially if both adults would really like things to improve.

Guideline seven: Remain available without prying. Children sometimes give their parent answers he or she wants to hear. They can figure out what the parent is looking for. If one parent is looking for evidence that the other is a jerk, the kids will feed that desire. The parental attitude must be, "Tell me your thoughts; I can handle them," regardless of what those thoughts may be.

Guideline eight: Handle visitation issues directly with the ex-spouse. It is never wise to send messages to the ex-partner through the kids. If you want that person to know something, contact him or her directly.

Guideline nine: Children need "moms" and "dads." Generally, it is best to encourage children to call step-parents "mom" and "dad." Kids won't forget who the "real" parent is.

Guideline ten: The natural parent must back the step-parent in discipline completely. The parent must let the child know that his or her new spouse is a lifetime partner.

In talking with our kids about divorce, we might take note of how this mother counseled her daughter Lisa:

MOM: "So, Lisa, do you think you'll be affected by Dad's and my divorce, or will it have no effect on you, or what?"

LISA: "I think it's pretty bad."

MOM: "Oh, really? Why's that?"

LISA: "I don't want you to get divorced from Dad.

MOM: "Oh, why is that? You know we fought all the time."

LISA: "Yeah, but I try to be good so you won't fight."

MOM: "Do you think we're fighting over you not being good, or do we fight over other things?"

LISA: "I don't know."

MOM: "Well, I want you to know that your dad and I do fight a lot, but frankly, most of it isn't over you. I think we'd be getting a divorce even if we'd never had children. You know this divorce makes me feel troubled. But just because it upsets me, does that mean it has to upset you, too? Or are you going to decide by yourself how much it upsets you?"

LISA: "I don't want you to be upset."

MOM: "Well, I am, honey. I thought I would be married to your dad for life. But you'll still get to see him a lot anyway. So, you don't have to be upset just because I'm upset. Because who was going to live with him his whole life? I was, right? That was never the plan for you. So I *should* be more upset about it."

LISA: "I was only going to live with him until I was eighteen?"

MOM: "Right. So, the main thing is, I don't want you to feel troubled just because I'm upset. You can decide for yourself how you're going to feel. What should you think about more — the divorce or your school work?"

LISA: "My school work."

MOM: "That would be great."

The message divorcing parents should send to their kids is, "This isn't going to wreck your lives. I know you can handle it. It might be hard, but now you may have three or four adults who love you instead of only two." Kids whose parents divorce have a much easier time if the parents are positive.

Pearl 13

❖

EATING AND
TABLE MANNERS

Lani, a loving mom, has spent the better part of her afternoon stooped over a hot stove. But that's all right, it's a special day. She's whipping up a treat, something new—chicken cacciatore—a dish never before seen on the family table. Sweat mingled with seasonings, labor with love. It made for a nice mix, she thought.

All eyes were on the proud chef as she carried her covered creation to the dinner table. She lifted the lid, savored the aromatic steam, and then awaited the gasps of appreciation from her loving children.

What does Lani hear instead? A chorus of "Oh, yuck! That stuff is gross!"

"Yuck" can spoil the dinner table joy, and when dinner table problems arise—either in displeasure with the food or with tacky table manners—the table becomes less an arena for love than a ground for battle.

But not to worry. Lani was a love-and-logic parent. She was disappointed, yes, but she took the criticism in stride. "No problem," she said as she scooped up her kids' plates and strode to the garbage disposal, where with one flip of the wrist the problem was resolved.

Then in a soft voice she said, "Run along, kids. Do what

kids do after dinner. We'll see you at breakfast."

Later on that evening, when hungry kids were raiding the refrigerator, Lani was up to the task then, too. She watched with curiosity, and when her kids had finished eating, she said, "You've just eaten $1.95 worth of food. How do you want to pay me—cash or from your allowance? The choice is yours." The logic behind her words is that she had already bought the food for the evening meal, and kids who rejected that meal and made their own must pay for it.

As with so many things, problems with eating can be eliminated when our kids are young through modeling and choices. Using thinking words instead of fighting words is helpful. Instead of saying, "You eat that and you eat all of it," or "I want that plate clean before you leave this table," the love-and-logic parent says, "Have you had enough to make it to the next meal? I hope so, but you decide."

Kids *should* be deciding how much they're going to eat. As they grow older, we won't be in a position to control what they put in their mouths, so the wise parent will ready them for the real world by allowing them to make decisions early.

To introduce new dishes, we may want to take a page from Carol's cookbook. Carol never had any problem getting her kids to eat what she wanted them to eat. Her recipe for success: Whenever she cooked anything new and different, she made only enough for two—her and her husband. The kids got hot dogs.

Then if they really liked it, the two adults lapped up the new dish as if it was the greatest thing ever to come off the top of a stove. "Oh, this is great!" her husband would exclaim. "I hope you cook this more often."

By the end of the meal, the kids would be saying, "Where's ours?"

Carol would say, "This is adult food. I don't know if you'd like this." And she wouldn't give them any.

Next night she served the same dish, and she and her

husband gobbled it up while raving even louder about how absolutely terrific it tasted. The kids would say, again, "Where's ours? We've got rights, too, you know."

But Carol kept control of the ladle. "It may be too rich for you," she said. "I think kids' taste buds just can't handle this sort of thing. You're probably not old enough."

By the third night, the kids were incensed. "We've got rights!" they demanded. "We want to have some, too!"

Then Carol relented. "Oh, all right," she said, doling out tiny portions onto their plates. "But don't eat too much." From then on Carol had few problems getting her kids to like what she prepared for dinner.

As for table manners, we fall back on the love-and-logic axiom: If you can't change the behavior, change the location. Even with the youngest children, we can nip tacky table behavior in the bud. A one-year-old who spits beets is given a choice: "Eat beets nice in your chair, or play on the floor."

With older kids we can vary the technique, allowing them to eat somewhere where they don't gross us out with their manners. When my (Foster's) wife is confronted with poor table manners, she dispatches the offending party with one sentence: "Take it to the dryer." Our kids won't gross anybody out but themselves while alone with their plates in the utility room.

Pearl 14

❖

FEARS AND MONSTERS

Monsters. Sometimes they're under the bed. Sometimes just outside the window. Sometimes they lurk under rugs or in closets, ready to spring out in gory horror the moment Mom leaves and extinguishes the last shaft of hallway light.

Unless you're a Big Foot believer, you'll agree that monsters lurk in children's heads, and there alone. Every kid, with his or her imagination at full throttle, knows that night creatures don't look like your basic friendly puppy.

One seven-year-old girl, after being adopted, imagined that her new parents only looked like humans, but at night their skin peeled off to reveal their true selves as lizards.

As silly as such fears seem to us as adults, they are very real to our kids, and may make some hesitate to crack the sheets. But vivid imaginations aside, monsters should not keep them from going to bed.

We must explore children's negative emotions (and their fears of going to bed) in a factual, understanding way without becoming emotionally involved. Our calmness rubs off on our children. Their problems usually become more severe if we become emotionally involved — that is, exasperated, angry, pleading, or frustrated.

An important rule of thumb applies: As soon as a conversation around a particular issue becomes predictable or the outcome predictably poor, the issue should *no longer be explored.*

Simple, calm reassurance that the child is competent to handle his or her own problem helps defuse the child's worry. Unfortunately, sometimes instead of giving simple reassurances, an *over*exploring or overly-involved parent may expand the problem. For example, pleading, "*Mary,* you'll be *all right,* honey," makes things much worse.

Also, the situation is not improved when we drop to our knees and personally check under the bed for monsters. Kids are likely to be more afraid, thinking, "Wow! Maybe there *are* monsters. Otherwise why would she be looking under the bed?"

We can also take advantage of magical thinking. Little kids really do believe in magic. Thus, it's very reassuring for little Ron to have a basic monster-chasing bear on his shelf. Sometimes only one molecule of mom's magic perfume on the upper left corner of the sheet definitely helps Naomi's sleep. Such techniques, of course, must be used in a light-hearted, caring way that takes advantage of the way kids naturally think. Furthermore, we should not make too big a deal of such practices. If we don't overly invest in such ploys, they will naturally be discarded as a child matures.

It's worth a few more pennies of electricity to allow night lights in the hall or bathroom. We can give in on this issue and *not give in* on allowing the child to enter our bedroom to wake us because he or she is afraid. Waking parents up for that reason is a definite no-no.

A discussion we may use to help defuse the monster problem might go like this:

CHILD: "I don't want to go to bed, Mom. I'm afraid I
   might die tonight."

MOM: "Luckily, only one child in ten million will die
in his sleep tonight, honey."
CHILD: "But I'm afraid."
MOM: "What are you afraid of?"
CHILD: "Monsters."
MOM: "Oh, I wouldn't worry about that. You have
Teddy with you."
CHILD: "Can you sprinkle some magic perfume on
my covers?"
MOM: "Sure."

Parents who defuse the monster problem by not making a big deal about it, or by not encouraging their children's
imaginations, will eventually have kids who go to bed without complaint when they get sleepy.

Pearl 15

◆

FRIENDS

Friends. From the time our kids get off the knees of infancy and onto the land legs of toddlerhood, they're going to be around other kids. Playing with dolls. Shooting baskets. Swapping baseball cards. Running in the neighborhood.

Our kids are going to make friends. That's the good news. As we know, friends are great for kids to have. The bad news is that often we don't like the friends they choose.

One of the biggest mistakes we parents make is getting into a control battle with our kids over who their friends are. We'll lose that one every time. Since we can't win that battle, we should keep our mouths shut and take a different tack. We should concentrate on the areas we can control.

We can offer our kids a choice: pick friends we approve of and then play with those friends at our house; or pick friends that we don't approve of and then make sure they never come near the house. Or we can say, "Would you like to have friends that really test your decision making and thinking skills, or would you rather have some that don't pressure you so much?"

The key relationship in discussing our kids' friends with them is the one between us and our kids. That must be preserved. When we try to change our kids' relationships, it may damage our own relationship with our children. Our kids rebel against our demands and orders.

Prohibiting our kids from playing with certain friends tells them we are afraid the friends' attitudes, beliefs, or habits will rub off. It also tells our kids that they can't do their own thinking. The result is usually that the friends become more exciting and desirable.

But we can tell them what we think. Children cannot rebel against thoughts and opinions. In fact, if our relationship with our kids remains communicative, in the long run our kids will generally pick friends we like.

Joan is about to leave the house for a rendezvous with friends of hers that her father doesn't approve of.

JOAN: "Bye, Dad. I'm leaving."

DAD: "Wait a minute. Let's have a goodbye kiss."

JOAN: "Oh . . . okay."

DAD: "Are you going out with Jean and Debby?"

JOAN: "Yeah. . . . So?"

DAD: "So . . . great! I'm just hoping, dear, that some of you rubs off on them."

JOAN: "Oh, Dad."

DAD: "Honey, I'm serious. Sometimes I just think those kids need you around them. Maybe you're a good influence on them or something."

JOAN: "You don't like them."

DAD: "It's not a matter of not liking them, Joan. I just worry sometimes that life may not go as smoothly for those kids as I hope yours goes for you. . . . Now, run along and have a good time."

We may be pleasantly surprised when we get to know our children's friends. Our kids often see good in others that we simply don't see. When we get to know our kids' friends, we may get to know more about our kids, too; we may understand why they're attracted to certain people.

Pearl 16

❖

GETTING READY
FOR SCHOOL

"How many times do I have to call you?" "You get yourself moving!" "You're going to be late for school if you don't step on it!" How often do we find ourselves barking these commands in the morning? And with good reason, we think. Our morning timetable is tight, the ritual complex. Unfortunately, many times, our children move about as fast as the continental drift in their preparations for school.

However, the first hour of the day is the very best time to teach kids responsibility. We do this by allowing them to do most of the thinking, and most of the jobs we usually do for them. These four general rules will make morning a friendlier time for all.

First, decide which jobs belong to the parents and which belong to the youngsters. A talk with the kids will help them see that setting the alarm, waking up to the alarm, choosing clothes, dressing, washing up, watching the clock, remembering lunch money and school supplies, and even deciding how much to eat, are really their responsibilities. The only people to suffer consequences if these are neglected are the youngsters. Our responsibility is to back up the school's consequences for lateness.

Second, stay out of the reminder business. Reminders

rob kids of the opportunity to make the mistakes needed to learn the lessons.

Third, don't rescue! Rescuing children robs them of the opportunity to learn lessons at emotional times when the lessons will be best remembered. In other words, if the kids walk to school, no taking them in the car so they won't be late. And no notes excusing their tardiness!

Finally, replace anger with sadness when they make mistakes. Wise parents, when seeing that their kids will be late, say, "Oh, honey, I'm sorry you're going to have a problem with your teacher. I sure hope you work it out."

This dialogue shows how to discuss the getting-up-on-time issue with our kids:

DAD: "What time does the school bus come in the morning, Mark?"

MARK: "8:20."

DAD: "So, what time do you want to get up?"

MARK: "Oh, eight."

DAD: "Great. How are you going to get up?"

MARK: "You'll come and wake me."

DAD: "Well, I always used to do that. But now that you're eight years old, I've realized I haven't been fair to you waking you up in the morning because a lot of kids your age wake themselves up. So, how do you think you'll wake yourself up?"

MARK: "My alarm clock."

DAD: "Good idea. You can set the alarm and get up at eight."

MARK: "What if I sleep through it?"

DAD: "Well, you'd probably end up missing school."

MARK: "Oh, good!"

DAD: "If you don't get up in time to meet the bus, you can spend the day in your room. Mom and I will just pretend you're at school. Don't come out of your room into the rest of the house until school's out. And you might want to spend some of that time thinking about how you will handle explaining your absence to your teacher."

MARK: "That's easy, you can write an excuse for me."

DAD: "I'll be glad to write the truth, that you are having a hard time getting yourself to school and that I will back the school on its punishment."

MARK: "But if I keep missing school, they might fail me!"

DAD: "I suppose they might. That would be sad for you."

Chances are, Mark will be up and waiting for the school bus when it rolls around the next morning. Kids with parents who are less concerned about their flunking and more concerned about giving their kids an opportunity to think about flunking develop kids who think and rarely flunk. Their parents aren't going to worry about it, so they'd better.

Occasionally our children's morning tardiness affects others too, as when we must drop them off at school or daycare on our way to work. Handling this dilemma takes a little inventiveness.

Five-and-a-half-year-old Steve made his mother late for work regularly. "It's not my fault I'm late," she would say. "Steve's never ready." She tried all the standard tactics to get him to be ready: spanking; taking things away; denying television privileges. Nothing worked.

Then she decided to give Steve some control. She said, "Steve, I'm so excited. Starting tomorrow, I'm never going to be late for work again because my car will leave every morning at 7:30, and there are two ways for you to go with me. Would you like to hear what they are?"

Steve said, "I guess so."

"Well," Mom said, "dressed is one way and not dressed is the other."

Come morning, Steve—who was not ready to change his behavior that easily—continued his go-slow campaign. He wasn't ready at 7:30. Mom came into his room and said, "You're not dressed, but that's no problem. You probably didn't feel like dressing. That's why I have this nice little bag. We'll just put your clothes in here. You can dress whenever you feel like it."

She took Steve by one hand and the bag by another, and out to the car they went. As she drove off she said, "I'm glad I'm going to be to work on time today."

Now, the Steves of this world are not going to take this lying down. They've got spunk. Steve took his best shot—right at Mom's jugular. "You don't love me," he wailed. "You put me in the back seat of the car with my pajamas still on."

Then Steve unveiled the rest of his arsenal. He kicked the back of the seat, squirmed around, and yelled. Soon he was waving to passing motorists like he'd been kidnapped. Eventually, a sad little voice in the back seat was heard: "I guess I'll just have to be dressed on time after this."

It might be necessary, when using this approach, to contact the child's teacher or the daycare superintendent beforehand. Instruct that person not to let the child into the room to participate in activities until he or she has his or her clothes on.

Pearl 17

---❖---

GRADES AND
REPORT CARDS

"Wendy doesn't understand math very well. We're kind of worried. We talked to her teacher. We spend hours on the problems every night, but we still get Cs and even Ds. And on our first report card we had a D+. I don't know how we're going to get through the second grade."

Wendy's twin sister talking? Guess again. It's Wendy's *mother*.

This is the cardinal rule for grades and report cards: Parents don't get report cards, kids do. The children sit in class. The children receive the instruction. The children do the work. And the children get the grade. For parents to be effective in dealing with the report card issue, they must *keep the monkey on the kids' back*.

It is important that children know that the report card is their business. As parents, we care. Our caring might even shade into concern. But solving the problem? That's our children's business.

I (Foster) remember vividly how my wise dad always kept the report card problem on my back. As a kid in elementary school, I had a very difficult time getting started in school. Once I came home with straight Ds. My dad looked over the report card, took out his fat, black fountain pen, and paused. "Son, are you proud of this?" he asked.

I answered, "No, sir."

"That's good, son," then my father signed the report card. This ritual occurred time and again. Thank goodness I never said I was proud of the report card. I would have had tutoring, private schooling, and heaven knows what all.

Problems with our kids' report cards can be measured with an algebraic equation based on feelings and performance. This formula lets us know when to be concerned:

- ◆ When a child does good work (+) and feels good about it (+), the result is positive (+ × + = +).
- ◆ When a child gets a good grade (+), but even then feels bad about himself or herself (−), the long-term outcome may be poor, in spite of the grade (+ × − = −).
- ◆ When a child does poorly (−) and feels bad about doing poorly (−), parents need not worry because things will eventually work out well (− × − = +).
- ◆ When a child does poorly (−) but feels fine about doing poorly (+), the result is negative (− × + = −).

In sum, when kids perform like turkeys but want to become eagles, they fly like pros. But when they perform like turkeys and feel like eagles, they never get off the ground.

With report cards, as with many other issues, children want pizzazz. They want parental emotion. On an unconscious basis, it doesn't matter whether the parental emotion is positive or negative. They'll shoot for it, regardless. Thus, when children return from school offering a report card of mixed quality, parents should enthuse over the positive and be nonemotionally insistent about the negative. A discussion might go like this:

DAD: "Hey, a big A in art! That's great! You always did like art, didn't you?"

CHILD: "Yeah, art is fun."

DAD: "And a B in gym. Well, of course, you always did run like the wind. And another B in music. That's really good. Hm-m-m, a D in math. Well, I suppose that could be better. Wow, a big B in social studies. It's important to know history and geography. (Then, nonemotionally) How are you going to handle the math?"

We should always get involved in the areas in which our children excel. If Becky does well in science, we spend some time together at the pond looking at critters through the microscope. If it's math that Mandy's good at, we find out if the harmonics of the solar system interest her. If history turns Allen's head, we explore books that present it in a colorful and interesting way.

When poor grades are discussed, talk in a nonemotional but caring manner: "Do you have any plan for history?" "What are your thoughts about the math grade?" "Do you think the science grade will get better with time, or will it probably continue to go downhill?" It is important that the questions do not take on a "witness stand" approach.

In reality, poor grades are not the problem. The reason for the poor grades is. Children get poor grades because of poor self-image, rebelliousness to the parental value system, anxiety, depression, learning problems, and a host of other reasons. Sometimes there is an attitude problem.

Some of these reasons may call for a different response. It may be beneficial to have an outsider look at the child's situation and help the parents decide on an appropriate reaction.

Pearl 18

❖

GRANDPARENTS

Summertime. Family reunions. Grandpa and Grandma and Mom and Dad and the kids. Rare and wonderful moments often transpire between grandparents and their grandchildren during these family get-togethers — and between the grown children and their parents as well.

Sadly, oftentimes the parent-child relationship is stressed by the behavior of our kids when they're around us and our parents at the same time. Usually kids are fine when alone with one or the other. But put the three generations together and it can be spontaneous combustion. The reason for this is that we sometimes raise our kids differently than the way we were raised, especially if we were raised with techniques different from love-and-logic parenting.

Grandparents may not understand what is going on between us and our kids. We react to our kids' mistakes with sadness rather than anger; we show kindness rather than protection; we're concerned but not worried. Generally, we give our kids responsibility, allowing for failure — knowing that the price tags of failure may be affordable and the children will learn great lessons from their experiences.

In more cases than not, our parents handled us entirely differently. Grandparents who do not understand these techniques may become critical and accusatory: "How could you let that happen to Drew?" they say. And tension within the relationship arises.

Before looking at techniques to avert this tension, we should remember that the model we set with our own parents will be followed by our children as they grow into adulthood. In the way that we treat our parents, so too will we be treated by our kids. (Has a shudder run up your spine?)

Second, remember that in a few unhappy cases, parents and children have had a downright toxic relationship. Adult children are sometimes drawn to their parents like moths to a flame—forever being burnt but forever returning, always hoping for a close relationship that will never occur. Clashes over raising the grandchildren are just symptoms of deeper, long-term problems.

Except for a few fortunate souls, most of us need to realize that we will go through life never being totally accepted or unconditionally loved by our parents, and all the energy spent trying to make it happen will only end in more frustration. This is important to remember as we discuss the four basic rules for parent-grandparent interaction.

Rule one: When we are together with our parents, it must be decided who is going to control the child. Usually, it should be the parents. If a grandparent feels the need to discuss a child's behavior, we should ask them to do so when the child is not misbehaving or present. A good way for them to present their thoughts is, "My relationship with you is really important, and I don't want to do anything that stresses it. I have some observations on the grandchildren. Would you like to hear them?" Only if we say yes, should the grandparent proceed.

Rule two: We should be assertive about our wishes. Rather than reacting to what grandparents say, it is best for us to actively look at the process of how things might be handled. For instance, we might say to our parent, "Mom, before you comment or talk to me about how I raise the children, I hope that you will first inquire about it lovingly and ask me why I am handling things the way I do. Does this sound reasonable to you?"

Rule three: Let the grandparents know why we are with them. Is it because of a sense of guilt or obligation? Or do we visit because we want to have fun? Sometimes we need to tell our parents, "Mom and Dad, people get together on vacations either out of a sense of obligation and guilt *or* to have fun together. I'm wondering if you see our times together as fun. If not, what do you see as the solution to this? Because I'm unwilling for us to relate purely out of a sense of obligation and guilt."

Rule four: Clarify bottom-line expectations. It is important that a few things be made clear to both parties. One request we must make of our parents is that they do not comment negatively on our parenting techniques in front of our children. Another might be that they not discipline the kids without our permission. In some cases, it might be necessary to discuss the option of leaving the kids at home so grandparents won't be tempted to meddle.

Likewise, grandparents have rights. If the kids are acting like hellions, grandparents have the right to either ask us to handle it or ask the entire tribe to leave.

If our parenting techniques are decidedly different from those of our folks, it might be wise to explain the principles of love-and-logic parenting before we visit.

In summary, the guidelines for handling grandparents are similar to those for handling children. Be assertive. Take care of yourself in a healthy way. Concentrate on problem solving rather than frustration and anger. And provide consequences if necessary.

Pearl 19

❖

HOMEWORK

Our kids' homework is their problem. It's their pencils that have to move, their minds that must be stretched, and their report cards that have to be toted home.

Far too many parents get sucked into the trap that somehow their children's schoolwork is the *parents'* problem. They hang ultimatums over their kids' heads. They condition completed homework on whether their kids are permitted to go out and play or watch television. They deprive and threaten and scream and shout. And if the homework is not done and the grades are not good, they lower the boom.

Our parental responsibility is to provide our kids with the *opportunity* to do their homework. Whether it be for a half-hour or an hour or even an hour-and-a-half, our children must sit down at a table or desk with their schoolbooks nearby. That's the opportunity. We allow the kids to choose the place (dining room, kitchen, or their room) and time. We even allow them to choose *whether* to study or not.

After all, there are two ways to learn. They can learn by doing their homework (i.e., reading and writing), or they can learn by thinking about doing their homework. Either way, they'll learn—although the lessons will be different.

Their teachers at school, who mete out the consequences, might not accept the second way of learning.

Rachel effectively handled the homework issue with her son Sean in this way:

> RACHEL: "Well, Sean, it's time for the homework hour. We've set aside this hour for you to do your homework. Are you ready?"
>
> SEAN: "Aw, Mom, do I have to?"
>
> RACHEL: "Well . . . you can learn either by doing your homework or by thinking about your homework. Which do you want to do tonight?"
>
> SEAN: "I'll just think about doing my homework."
>
> RACHEL: "You can do it that way if you want, son. I hope you'll be able to get your teacher to go along with it. Do you think he'll accept that method of doing homework?"
>
> SEAN: "I don't know."
>
> RACHEL: "Well, why don't you give that some thought before you think about your homework tonight. You've got a lot of thinking to do in an hour. So, I'll see you when you're done."

There is nothing wrong with parents helping their kids with homework. Many children want help, and we should be there with the needed hint or explanation. But only if our kids ask for it, and only as long as it's profitable. When we start to become irritated, we've helped enough.

In this way, we present our children with a positive role model by not allowing *their* problem with homework in an unhealthy way to become our problem. But our positive model shouldn't stop there. We show our kids the proper way to approach homework when we talk about the importance of doing our own homework or office work. Saying things like, "I've got to get my homework done," immediately after dinner, or "I don't feel good doing anything else until I get my work done first," then following through gives our kids an example to imitate.

Unwillingness to do homework is a complicated issue. Laziness is only one cause. A myriad of other underlying causes may be at the core of the problem. The child might have a learning disorder, a neurological problem, an attention-deficit problem, or an attitude problem. In these cases, treating the symptoms does no good whatsoever. If you determine that these more serious underlying causes exist, seek professional counseling.

Pearl 20

❖

"I'm Bored" Routine

It's three hours after the dawn of Christmas morning and calm has replaced flying paper and frantic squeals of delight. Toys, toys, and more toys litter the floor—enough diversion to keep three daycare centers going for years. Then from the rubble, a sad little face emerges and a doleful voice is heard, "Mommy, I'm bored."

Our inevitable response is, "What? Bored? You've got more toys than all the kids in the Third World put together, and you're bored? No. It's a psychological impossibility."

Bored kids put the dread in the first day of summer vacation. Continual cries of "Daddy, what can I do?" make us long for the day when the big yellow buses resume their daily rounds.

Despite what our kids say, they probably aren't bored. When children say they are bored, it usually means "I want you to spend more time with me."

Playing with our kids is one of the great joys of parenting. But when we agree to do so, we should make it plain to them that their boredom is their problem. The parent in the following discussion handled the problem well:

CHILD: "I'm bored. There's nothing going on around here."

PARENT: "Are you really bored? That's too bad. What are your plans?"

CHILD: "Well, what can I do?"

PARENT: "That is a really good question. What kinds of things are in your room?"

CHILD: "Aw, there's nothing in there that I like. I'm tired of it all."

PARENT: "Well, are there things that you like anywhere else in the house?"

CHILD: "I don't think so."

PARENT: "A lot of people get involved with things that they like so they won't be bored. You're saying that, when you're bored, there's nothing you really like?"

CHILD: "Right."

PARENT: "So, it looks to me like there may not be any other option than to sit and be bored. Would you say that was a possibility?"

CHILD: "I guess I could play with my video game."

PARENT: "Would you like me to play one game with you?"

CHILD: "Yeah!"

PARENT: "I guess I could play one game. But if I do that, do you think you'll say, 'Oh, thank you,' or will you whine and say, 'Oh, please, play one more'? How will you handle it if I play one game with you?"

CHILD: "I promise not to ask for another game."

We want our kids to develop the ability to motivate, interest, and entertain themselves. Allow them to poke their way out of their self-imposed shell of boredom, rather than providing them with an entertainment service.

Pearl 21

❖

Lying and Dishonesty

Most children, from kindergarten through about the second grade, go through a lying stage. They may be very unskilled with their fibbing, or they may be as clever as Joe Isuzu. But they're lying all the same.

Dishonesty can turn parents purple with frustration. After all, who wants to raise kids with integrity problems? But we are often at a distinct disadvantage because, frankly, we don't know if they're telling the truth or not!

If we catch them in the act, that's one thing. But if we merely suspect fibbing, all of our investigative questioning, done when our kids might be telling the truth, may breed a self-fulfilling prophecy. It's been said that if we wrongly accuse our kids twice for the same thing, they'll set out to prove us right. You can almost hear them say with a sigh, "You think I do it anyway, so I might as well do it." That does not mean, however, that we can't discuss lying with our children. Some healthy doubt is okay.

When talking to our kids about a suspected lie, make sure they're doing the thinking. One effective technique goes like this: "Do you think I believe you right now, or do you think I don't believe you?" If our kids respond with "But, I'm telling the truth," we should resist taking an accusatory tone. Calling children liars is like throwing a grenade at a squad of Green Berets. Kids will fight back — insisting that they're telling the truth — simply to protect themselves.

If we think a child is lying, it's better to say, "If it's the truth and I don't believe you, then that's sad for both of us. But if it's a lie and I don't believe you, then it's double sad for you." First, the child is telling a lie, and second, he or she is around people who don't believe him or her.

Many parents run scared from saying, "I don't believe you" to their kids. They fear that saying it will somehow destroy the bond of mutual trust. But the phrase is useful. Kids don't have a comeback to it — they can only defend their honesty. We're not calling them liars; we're simply stating that we don't believe them. That makes *them* do the thinking.

However, if we know our child is lying — if we've caught him in the act — then the dialogue is over. We say, "Ken, you *did* hit Doug in the face. No matter what you say, I saw you do it. Now how are you going to make it right?" The act has occurred, the child is guilty. The only question is: What is the child going to do about it?

Generally, honesty is conveyed to our kids through our actions, not our commands. We need to step back and analyze the model we are presenting our kids. Do we ever ask our kids to lie for us? Have we ever whispered into our children's ears "I'm not home" when somebody we don't want to talk to calls on the phone? Do our kids ever see one parent call in sick for the other parent, just because Dad or Mom doesn't want to go to work that day? Have we made up lame excuses (translated, lies) to get out of social or church obligations? These things may be little, true, but they have more impact on our kids than all the lectures about honesty we could ever deliver.

When kids do tell the truth, love-and-logic parents respond with support. We must say, "Thank you for being honest. I'm sure it was hard for you to tell me that. I bet it was hard on you to know you made that mistake. That is really sad." Then we drop the issue.

Too many parents tell their kids, "It's better for you if you tell the truth," then they punish their kids for what they did wrong. Such a statement might be true in the long run, but most kids see life through short-run eyes. If they are grounded for a month in punishment for a "crime," it is clearly *not* better for them to tell the truth the next time.

Rather, we should be more sad for our kids than angry. The consequences will do the teaching, not some unrelated punishment we might impose.

Pearl 22

❖

Nasty Looks and Negative Body Language

"Every time I ask Pam to do something, or even sometimes when I want to talk to her, it happens," one mom said. "She slumps her shoulders and kind of tilts her head a little. Then she gives me this look that could open oysters at fifty paces. It really inflames me, and I don't know what to do about it."

Negative body language: Those irritating little shows of displeasure our children throw at us whenever we ask them to do something they don't want to do, or talk about something they don't want to talk about. The rolling of the eyes, the look of disgust, the stomping off, the slamming of doors. These nonverbal messages say *something*, that much we know. Our question as parents is: What?

Most parents believe their children are copping an attitude on them—a bad attitude. But what does Pam really mean when she fires that icy glare at her mom? Is she disappointed, or angry at herself, or trying to say that Mom's unfair, or saying that she feels hurt or let down or criticized? Pam's mom doesn't know for sure, and oftentimes, neither do we.

The best response is to say what we have to say, and then walk away. Negative body language is not a problem

173

for us if we don't acknowledge it. But if it continues, we may want to deal with it. And that means thinking of our own behavior. What did we do or say the instant before our child shot his or her eyes toward the sky? Did we criticize our child? Is he or she merely responding to that criticism? Kids are like adults when it comes to taking criticism — they react to it, often in a negative way. Then, when emotions have cooled and both we and our children are reasonably happy, we can attempt to get at the root of the problem.

> MOM: "Hey, Pam, is this a good time to talk?"
>
> PAM: "Yeah, I guess so."
>
> MOM: "I've noticed that sometimes when I say something to you, you give me a certain look, and I have a hard time understanding what that really means. You know, some kids do that because they don't feel it's safe to say that they're hurt or disappointed. Some kids do that because they're unhappy. Other kids do it because they hate their mom and wish she would shut up. Do you have any thoughts on that?"
>
> PAM: "No."
>
> MOM: "That might explain a lot . . . the fact that you don't have any thoughts on it. I sure would like to hear about it if you do. Why don't you give it some thought? One thing I'm thinking is that maybe I'm doing something to make you feel bad or criticize you or something. If you feel like you're up to telling me something about that, I'd sure be a good listener."

Then Mom should drop the issue and see what happens.

Pouting is another nonverbal sign of displeasure. Kids use it to beg their parents to talk to them. Once we have taken the bait by either asking what is wrong, or telling them to get rid of that look, we are doomed. The children now have us as a captive audience. Often, it is effective to say, "Well, it looks like things are not going well for you right now. When you get yourself to the point of putting your thoughts into words, come and talk to me. I'll be glad to listen." Then break eye contact and move on.

If the negative body language is such a constant that we can successfully predict when it will happen, we might preface our remarks to our child with a comment like, "Hey, Pam, I have something I want to share with you. Now, when I get through you may want to melt me with that laser look you're so good at, so get it ready." It's hard for kids to do something we have given them permission to do; they don't feel as if they're in control.

When we consider the range of options open to our kids when they're unhappy with us—everything from ignoring us to telling us where to go—the rolling eyes or the steely gaze aren't so bad. It gives our kids the chance to save face, a little room to retain some control. We all need that opportunity when placed in a situation we're not pleased with.

Pearl 23

❖

PEER PRESSURE

The battle over peer pressure begins when our children are two or three years old. That doesn't mean our diaper-clad youngster will toddle through the door tomorrow with a purple mohawk hairdo and a nail-studded motorcycle jacket. Kids are growing up quicker than ever before, but not *that* quick. It does mean that the battle of the dominant voices in each child's head starts in toddlerhood. Isn't that what peer pressure is all about—kids listening to the voices of their peers rather than thinking for themselves?

Many of us unwittingly train our children to listen to their peers by teaching them, while young, to listen to a very strong voice outside their own head—ours. We say, "Do what I tell you to do, do it now, and do it my way."

When these children hit adolescence, a very profound shift in their thinking occurs. They say, "I can now think for myself. I don't have to listen to that strong voice outside my head." So they begin to think for themselves, right? Wrong. Consider their quandary. They've been conditioned for eleven years to listen to our voice. They're not going to listen to us anymore (they've decided that), and they can't listen to a voice inside of their own heads (there isn't any;

176

we've done all their thinking for them). So, the only voice that registers is their peers' — another voice coming from outside their heads.

Many of us throw up our hands in frustration when our children hit eleven or twelve years of age, saying, "My kids used to listen to me, but now they won't. Boy, have they ever changed." Wrong, again. They haven't changed one iota. They're still listening to a voice outside their heads. It's just not ours.

The first step in preparing our children to cope with the peer pressure they'll meet down the road is to start them early listening to a small voice inside their own heads. Give them choices on little things: Chocolate or white milk? The blue coat or the red coat? Put the mittens in the pocket or wear them? They have to decide; the little voice inside their head does the talking.

The more decisions kids make, the more times we ask them questions instead of telling them what to do, the more we discuss issues using thinking words, the less likely they'll be negatively influenced by peers later on.

We shouldn't fool ourselves, however. *Peer pressure will still be strong.* During those early preadolescent and adolescent years they're trying so hard to build social skills, and friendships will be crucial. But with good preparation, their own inner voice will have a fighting chance.

Second, when our children hit eleven or twelve, to prepare them to cope with peer pressure, it is essential that we have little discussions with them from time to time about the pressures of adolescent life. For example:

DAD: "Kristin, I know how hard it is to be facing
adolescence now, and how important your friendships are to you. Mom and I want to support
you in your friendships and everything else you
may be going through. I just want to have a little
talk today to see how that's going for you and

whether you're able to think when you're around
your friends or not. Okay?"
KRISTIN: "Uh, okay, I guess."
DAD: "I thought maybe we could talk about your
plan for making sure you get to be yourself.
Because I know you're working very hard not to
be your parents. So, the next job is to learn how
not to be your friends, too, and instead to become
yourself."

Another fruitful area of discussion involves the concept
of saying no. Will our children be able to say no to their
friends? If we have allowed the voice inside their heads to
gain in volume and quality over the years, they will. But we
should teach our kids to say no to their peers just like we
say no to *them*: by saying yes to something else. If friends
want them to try drugs (this can happen before they hit
their teens, by the way), it's easier for them to decline the
offer by saying, "Hey, I'd be glad to go roller skating or
to the mall or to the yogurt shop. I want to do something
with you, but I'd like it to be something other than drugs."
Kids feel a lot stronger when they know how to say yes to
something else rather than just saying no and feeling "out
of it" and alone.

It also helps if we offer ourselves as fall guys. We
should tell our children, "If you need to say no to a peer
and you want to use us as the bad guys, feel free to say,
'No, my folks would kill me if I did that!' We'll back you
up." This is one additional tool we can give our kids.

Pearl 24

❖

PET CARE

Our pets are there when we need them, providing companionship and love. And they're consistent, they seem to always be *up*—except for cats, who can figure them out?

Pets provide our kids with a wonderful opportunity to learn responsibility. Most of us agree to take pets into our homes with the proviso that they are our kids' responsibility. Our kids must feed and water them, clean their messes, and tend to their houses, cages, or tanks. But all too often, we end up trudging along behind Fifi with the pooper scooper or transferring Goldie and Hawn into a mixing bowl so we can scrub the rocks from their fish tank.

It doesn't have to be like that. We can keep the responsibility of pet care on our children's shoulders, but it takes real parental chutzpah.

One mother of two girls lived by the mealtime motto "I only feed four mouths." If her daughters hadn't fed the family's cat and dog by 5:00 p.m., then the four mouths were Mom, Dad, cat, and dog. "You're not eating dinner tonight," Mom would explain to her daughters, "because I used my energy feeding Charlemagne and Fred." Then she would give her daughters a kiss on the cheek, a smile and a hug, and say, "We're sure going to miss you at the dinner table."

179

If that technique doesn't get results, then wise parents will attempt to find the pet a different owner. Explaining kindly and without criticism to the children, "Buster really needs somebody who will feed him on a regular schedule," or "Budgee needs someone who will always clean the cage because he really must have his cage cleaned." Then give the animal away.

The other alternative is to take care of the pets ourselves. But if our children know that Smokey will be fed by Mom, or Rodent's cedar chips will be changed by Dad, they'll cease to worry about Smokey or Rodent. Pet care is then our problem, not theirs. The choice is ours.

Pearl 25

❖

PICKING UP BELONGINGS

The unofficial world record for trashing a living room was set in early 1987 by a Colorado lad named Tommy: Forty-five seconds. In under a minute, this five-year-old tornado had bounced seventeen teddy bears down two flights of stairs and scattered three cylinders of Lincoln Logs, two complete sets of Legos, four boxes of Crayola 64s, and enough plastic army men to invade the next county. By the time he'd dumped his big sister's 500-piece puzzles, you couldn't even see the carpet.

"Not a bad minute's work," Tommy said to himself as he surveyed his handiwork. "But it's sure too messy in here to play. I'm going down to the basement."

Kids and their toys. We can be sitting in relative order one minute, but let kids loose with their belongings and before we can turn a page in the evening paper, the room is trashed. Who puts in an hour or two of stoop labor cleaning it up? Us. It's a double whammy. We have to do the work, plus our children don't learn how to care for their belongings.

Modeling is the secret to instilling a sense of responsibility about personal belongings. Our kids will do as we do. Unfortunately, some parents can't blame their kids for not picking up their toys. Mounds of clothes drape the chairs of the master bedroom, and it took two hours to find the mower in the garage the last time the lawn needed a trim. These parents don't take care of their own belongings. As kids enter the stage in their lives when they want to be big and feel big, they imitate the big people in their lives — us.

In addition to caring for our own things, referential speaking also sends powerful messages. Talking to ourselves or to our spouse about how good we feel when we know our things are neatly put away tells our kids it's great to be neat. Putting the dishes away, replacing the tools on their proper hooks, sweeping the sidewalks after mowing the grass — if we're talking about it as we do it, and after we do it, our kids get the right message.

Until our kids hit kindergarten, cleaning up their toys should be a community project. We put away a toy, then they put away a toy, then we put away a toy, and so on. After that age, however, their toys are their responsibility. What happens to them is up to the kids.

If they leave them laying around their room, that's one thing. We don't make a big issue out of it. But if every time we take a step across the family room we stub our toes on a toy truck, that's another. One parent handled the issue like this:

> PARENT: "Hey, Peter, there's a lot of your stuff laying around the house today. It's kind of getting in the way. Do you want to pick it up, or would you rather I picked it up?"
>
> PETER: "You pick it up."
>
> PARENT: "Well, the advantage of your picking it up is that you'll get to see it again. If I pick up, I'll keep the stuff. So you might want to rethink your decision on that. But you don't have to rush. I'll know what you want. If by lunchtime I still see your stuff out there, I'll know you decided to

have me pick it up. If I see that it's gone, then I'll
know that you decided to pick it up for yourself."

If we end up moving the toys, the question then
becomes, should we give them back to our child? That
depends on how generally responsible the child is. If our
child is basically responsible, then we'd say, "It's no problem. Every time you pick up all of your things by yourself
without being told, you earn back one of the toys you lost
today."

But kids who have a hard-core problem with responsibility should know that they are gradually saying bye-bye
to the toys we have to pick up. But don't feel too bad about
it. In most American homes, kids have far more toys than
they know how to take care of.

Also, don't be afraid of saying from time to time, "I'm
really worried about the way you're taking care of this or
that. I'm thinking maybe you need to be a little older before
you have that responsibility. So, I'm going to take that toy
until I don't have to worry about how well you're taking
care of it. You'll get another shot at it sometime. But don't
worry about it. There's no big hurry." There's no hurry for
us, that is. We aren't going to worry about that toy. But the
child will, and that translates into an attempt on their part
to be more responsible.

Pearl 26

---❖---

PROFESSIONAL HELP:
WHEN TO SEEK IT

A delicate question often arises from parents of troublesome children: "When should we decide to seek professional help?"

First, get it out of your head that seeking professional help is an admission of failure. In our complex society, with its myriad social problems, our kids quite naturally face dilemmas that we never had to cope with during our childhood. Societal pressures for success, for example, are overwhelming, filtering down even to the lower grades. Peer pressures prompt kids to insist on Calvin Klein jeans and Air Jordan sneakers—when they're still in kindergarten! More kids have severe problems than ever before, and the causes of those problems stand apart from the method or intent of parental discipline.

Thus, we offer two guidelines for the seeking of professional help:

1. If you have read this book—ingesting the love-and-logic philosophy and applying it to your children—and you still have big problems, then you need professional help.
2. If a situation has gotten progressively worse over a

three-month period, with no improvement in sight, you should seek out a counselor.

But be advised: Professional care does not necessarily mean a long drawn-out series of counseling sessions. Oftentimes, one session with a trained counselor who knows what he or she is talking about is enough to straighten the problem out.

Pearl 27

———————◆———————

THE ROOM:
KEEPING IT CLEAN

The eyes swivel furtively for a look down the hall. No footsteps. No voices. It *seems* safe. The hand creeps slowly, tentatively, to the doorknob, despite the ominous warnings posted all around: "No Trespassing," "Keep Out," "Enter at Your Own Risk."

Sometimes a mom must risk personal safety in pursuit of a greater cause—even if that cause is nothing more than curiosity. She turns the knob and waits. Nothing. No booby traps. No sirens. No Teenage Mutant Ninja Turtles lunging to grab her throat. A welcome breath of relief passes her lips.

Carefully, cautiously, she pushes open the door, shielding her eyes in preparation of the sight. But it is too much. She screams. Then the awful thud of a human body hitting the floor. Silence.

Entering a child's room can be hazardous to your health. The condition of that room—or the toxicity of the health hazard, as the case may be—can be cause for a great deal of parent-child friction. How much effort to expend on the "condition of the sty" really depends on the age and responsibility level of the child.

Toddlers and preschoolers can be taught the joy of having a clean room by parental example. Parents can join the child in cleaning the room, talking all the while: "Doesn't it feel good to get all twenty-five of your stuffed Snoopys in a row," or "I feel so much better now that I know you won't trip on those dust balls."

When we help our tykes clean their room, the unspoken message we send is that there's the job, there's fun, and there's us helping them. However, when our children hit the third grade, it's time to take one large step back—out of the picture. Then there's the job and there's fun, but no us. We relinquish control and allow our kids' room to be their own private domain.

The child's room is a great learning ground for irresponsible kids, though. If our kids are not at the level of responsibility they should be, we can take the large step back into the picture.

The state of our kids' room is a control battle we can win. But making an issue of it doesn't mean yelling at them. It means offering choices and using other love-and-logic techniques. Here again we want to avoid telling our kids when to clean their room. Much better is to set a certain time by which they must have it done. A conversation might go like this:

PARENT: "Would it be reasonable for you to have your room cleaned by Saturday morning when we're all going to the amusement park? Because everybody who has his or her room cleaned by then gets to go."

CHILD: "Aw, I don't want to clean my room."

PARENT: "Well, that's okay. You don't have to. You can hire me or your sister or your brother to do it. We'd love some extra cash."

CHILD: "But I don't have any money."

PARENT: "You know, when adults don't have any money, they sell something."

CHILD: "Sell something?"

PARENT: "You don't have to decide now what you're going to sell. You can tell me by Saturday. If you can decide by Saturday that means you get to choose what to sell. And if you can't, that means I choose. So you have a choice of who chooses. That's up to you."

Chances are, that child will decide to clean his or her room. But with average, responsible kids, if the room's a mess, so what? That room is their business. They have to store all the stuff they've accumulated in their entire lives within those four walls. Dolls, computers, basketballs, xylophones, skateboards, video games, 450 stuffed animals. Where's it all supposed to go?

Kids keep their room about as clean as we keep the garage—and for the same reason. It's a storage area. Maybe we should let them keep their room the way they want to.

Pearl 28

❖

THE ROOM:
KEEPING THE KID IN IT

 The relationship between kids and their room is a curious thing. As parents of teenagers know, sometimes the hardest thing in the world is to get them out of their room. For them it is a secret, private place, far removed from the turmoil of adolescent life. But when kids are little, the problem is different: they won't stay *in* their room.

Clara summed up her problem with little Brad: "When Brad is a nuisance to my ears, I follow the love-and-logic plan. I decide what's best for both of us. And if I can't change his behavior, I change the location. I pick him up and haul him to his room. But as soon as I let him down and walk down the stairs, there he is, following me."

Once we've sent our kids to their room, how do we make them stay there? Clara did one thing that we should avoid — physically carrying the child to his or her room. Except when our kids are very small, when we can put them in a crib, they should go to their room under their own power.

At around age two, a statement — "I want you to go to your room, and I want you to go now" — spoken firmly and with index finger pointing toward the room, will usually get results. If the child toddles back out, we administer a solid pop to the rear and ask him or her to go back. However, spanking should be used only for defiance of Basic German Shepherd commands (come, sit, go, no, stay), and then only when a child is less than three years old (see pearls 10, 11, and 31).

Sometimes kids want to leave their room because of some previous traumatizing experience, such as hospitalization or surgery. These children need our special understanding, and often a good discussion with much reassurance helps them overcome their fears. But knowing the reason for the problem is not an excuse to let it continue. If the behavior persists, we must allow them to work it out.

In addition to disciplinary situations, another major problem parents face is when children wander out of their room at night, waking their parents for drinks of water or because they're afraid. A night light may help cure this problem. If the child continues to pester parents at night (many kids will), a more direct solution is needed.

Set up an evening or two to deal with the problem. On that evening say to your spouse, within the child's hearing, "We need to get a good night's sleep and that's difficult to do with Bert around. How about you and me going to the Holiday Inn (or so and so's house) tonight? We'll be able to relax and get a good night's sleep." Then the parents would give Bert a loving kiss and hug and call a baby-sitter, whom they've notified earlier, to come stay with the youngster overnight.

The baby-sitter has a role to play, too. He or she should say things to the child like, "Looks like your parents need a good night's sleep. Maybe they only need one night, but they might need more." If the child wakes the baby-sitter in the middle of the night, he or she should be non-responsive: "I don't know what to do with kids who get up in the middle of the night because I don't have any kids who do that." The baby-sitter may have to do this two or three times during the night, but it's *absolutely important* that he or she not capitulate to the child's request.

Allow the baby-sitter to send the child off to kindergarten or preschool in the morning or, depending on how responsible the child is, to reinforce the notion that the child must get himself or herself off to school.

There should be no anger on the baby-sitter's part or yours. We blow it completely when we say, "Just see how you like spending the night without us in the house. How are you going to feel about that?" The child then becomes angry at us instead of concerned about his or her own problem. Phrases like "We have to leave the house," "You're making us leave," or "Look what you're making us do" also send the wrong message.

We leave the house for one reason only: we want to get a good night's sleep. Saying, "Honey, we need a good night's sleep, and we might have to leave home tonight to do that. We might want to do this a lot of other nights because it's really good for Daddy and me to get a good night's sleep. Sometimes we sleep better when we're away from you," usually swings it.

Many kids who get up in the middle of the night are dependent on their parents. Sometimes, the only way to cure this dependence is to not be there for them. This may seem like an extreme, complicated, and expensive solution, but if you're a parent who has not had a decent night's sleep for months or years, this approach is well worth the effort and cost. You can even do it for free, if friends with a similar problem want to trade houses for a night. Kids are reluctant to bug strange "parents"; they don't know which buttons to push.

Pearl 29

SASSING AND DISRESPECT

" I don't have to listen to you. So shut up!" If you've ever been downwind of an explosion of defiant words like these from your child's mouth, you probably know all about your reaction. Purple face. Clenched fists. Pursed lips. Maybe even a sprint for the paddle. And all of that is just a prelude to the fireworks that follow.

Disrespectful kids are tough to take. They seem to have a smart-aleck comeback for everything we say. The trouble is that when we detonate a fireworks display in response, we are actually rewarding our kids for sassing us. We are giving our children emotion. And kids thrive on parental emotion; they lean back and enjoy the show. It's a part of human nature. Sermons on fire and brimstone usually will outdraw those concentrating on Jesus' love. Humankind doesn't want peace; it wants emotion.

Rather than saying, "No child of mine is going to speak to me like that," followed by a sermon-length lecture on respect, love-and-logic parents make it clear from the start that sassing does not result in an emotional response. Words will fall on deaf ears when one or both of the parties in a discussion is angry.

Thus, we talk about sassing only when our kids *are not*

sassing us. The key to defusing sassy kids is to get them out of your sight and earshot until they can speak quietly and calmly and your blood pressure has dropped fifty points. But we don't dictate their exile. We let them pick the banishment of their choice: "Would you like to go to your room, or outside, or down to the basement? Come back when you can talk as calmly as I'm talking right now."

Observe how Suzanne handles her disrespectful son Calvin:

> CALVIN: "I don't have to listen to you. Shut up!"
> SUZANNE: "You know, Calvin, no one can make you listen. And I think right now we're having a hard time listening to each other. So why don't you go someplace else for a while?"
> CALVIN: "I don't have to go someplace else. This is my house, too, you know. I live here. Besides, you never listen to me."
> SUZANNE: "Calvin, I'll be glad to listen when you've calmed down. But now, I think you'd be a lot happier if you went someplace else."
> CALVIN: "You never listen to a word I say!"
> SUZANNE: "I think you'd be a lot happier if you went someplace else."
> CALVIN: "It's not fair!"
> SUZANNE: "Sorry you see it that way, but I think you'd be a lot happier if you went someplace else."

With sassy kids, use the broken-record routine. Getting them away from you until calmness sets in is the primary mission. But don't forget that discussion you promised. "Smart mouth" can be cured. When tempers have cooled and words can be spoken without a flush of color coming to anybody's face, try to discover the child's reason for being disrespectful.

At that point, it is useful to say, "Calvin, I notice that you often have words for me when I ask you to do things. I wonder if I'm hearing it the same way you mean it. I'm confused about what you're trying to tell me. Are you trying to tell me that you're embarrassed, or that you feel put down, or that you want to be the boss, or that you hate me, or that you just don't know a better way to answer, or what? Does anything sound familiar to you?" This usually leads to a discussion. It is absolutely essential that you listen without being defensive or judgmental. (Be ready to part ways again if you feel the emotions rising.) The reaction that works best is to say, "Thanks for sharing."

Pearl 30

❖

SIBLING RIVALRY AND FIGHTING

It never seems to fail. We can buy our sons enough toy trucks to start their own freight line, but when push comes to shove, one specific truck becomes the heart's desire of both boys. They tug and shove and shriek. They won't back down no matter what. It's a maddening phenomenon.

Normal parents who have normal kids have kids who fight. That's one of the things kids do. Sibling rivalry is a part of growing up. Unfortunately, many of us tell ourselves we're not good parents if our children fight. However, if that were the measure of good parenting, there wouldn't be a single good parent on the face of the earth.

The thing to remember about dealing with our kids' fights is to butt out of them. Expect them to handle it themselves. This may be the toughest parenting principle to follow, because kids desperately want our intervention. In fact, our intervention makes it safe for them to fight. They know we'll step in before anyone gets hurt, so they have no qualms about putting up their dukes.

Our involvement in these spats should involve only the location of the fight—somewhere away from us. As soon as the bickering starts to invade our ears, our kids are out of here. "Hey, guys, take it outside" is as effective a way of dealing with squabbles as anything.

Of course, we must step in if life and limb are in danger. If a big kid continually terrorizes a little kid—showing relentless anger toward him or her—then we need to stop it. Most of the time, however, we must remember that it takes two to tangle. Even the smallest and frailest of kids has ways to get to big brother or sister. They will submit to hours of punishment simply to watch two minutes of big brother or sister "getting it" from mom and dad. So, if the "pickee" eggs on the "picker" only about one-third of the time, then we should let them solve their own disagreements.

When the tongues have been stilled and fists unclenched, then and only then do we counsel our children about fighting. Trying to reason with kids who are emotionally upset is a waste of good air.

Helping our children solve their difficulties involves identifying their feelings. Were they feeling mad, sad, frustrated, left out, or something different? Why did they resort to angry words rather than playing nice? First, they need to identify their feelings, and second, they need to identify different ways of handling them.

We can use modeling at this point: "If I went and hit my boss, Mr. Jackson, whenever I felt frustrated, I probably wouldn't be as happy as if I handled my frustration another way." The point is, we must identify with the child's feelings, and then help the child work out a new course of action. However, with really ornery children—ones that glory in brutalizing their peers—it may be necessary to provide them with a significant learning opportunity.

I (Foster) once counseled a little boy named Kurt who was an expert at terrorizing other little kids. His *modus operandi* was simple yet effective: He simply aimed for them on the playground and then mowed them down.

Two weeks after I placed Kurt in one of my best foster homes, he and his foster mom came in for an appointment. The little lion had become a lamb. He gently held his foster mom's hand. Love bloomed between them. I asked, "Kurt, how's the fighting going these days?"

"Oh, I'm not fighting much anymore," Kurt said.

"Well, why not?" I asked. "That was your forte."

Kurt looked up at his mom and said, "Oh, because I hate doing all the chores."

I gave the boy a quizzical look. Kurt's rowdy behavior and doing chores didn't seem to connect in my mind. Kurt, seeing my perplexed look, explained: "Dr. Cline, when I fight, my mom says it drains energy from the family. But when I clean behind the refrigerator with a hand brush, that puts energy back into the family."

That explained it. In an untrained home, parents would have commanded Kurt to stop his behavior. They would have said, "Kurt, don't you beat up on that other kid or you'll regret it," and Kurt would have had his knees on the other kid's arms before they finished the sentence. But the foster mom had connected Kurt's behavior with a consequence. When Kurt's behavior deteriorated, she could look at him and say, "Kurt, honey, I feel an energy drain coming on," and Kurt would think, "Oh, no, not that!" and there would be no fight.

Pearl 31

❖

SPANKING

"Daddy, why can't we just have a spanking and get this over with?"

Six-year-old Tanya had just slipped quietly into the living room where Dad reads his paper. She begged, "Our friends get to have spankings . . . and then they get to play. If you give us a spanking, we'll never play in the street again. We're tired of waiting for you to decide what you're going to do."

"Yeah," thought Dad. "Spankings are a lot easier than having to wait and think about what you've done wrong. They give kids a quick escape from the responsibility of living with a bad choice. Instead of having to live with consequences and think about solutions, youngsters have a brief moment of pain . . . then they're off the hook."

The original editions of this book advocated the use of spanking in limited, controlled situations. However, as Foster and I have grown in our profession, and as more valid research has become available, we have changed our position.

There are many good reasons to avoid the use of spankings:

198

1. Empathy and logical consequences are far more powerful than spanking, because they teach problem-solving skills.
2. Spanking fails to teach the behaviors we want.
3. Most kids would rather receive a spanking than have to think about their poor choice.
4. More recent research tells us that spanking has many negative side effects, such as anger, resentment, revenge, etc.
5. Our kids may someday choose our nursing homes.

Love and Logic techniques often leave children wishing for spankings. Such was the case with Tanya, who begged her father, "Daddy, could we just have a spanking and get this over with? We're tired of waiting!"

I (Jim) was first introduced to this idea when a student from my school spilled the beans to his therapist. This wonderful counselor, using some reverse psychology, asked this boy, "Tony, do you *really* have to do what those teachers tell you? Maybe you can get by *without* following the school rules."

"Oh, no! Oh, no!" yelled Tony. "You have to do what they tell you! If you don't, you have to go to Mr. Fay's office and think! I'm not going through that again! No way!"

Unlike the previous principal, I refrained from using the paddle. The simple rule in my office was that kids had to solve the problems they created. They were constantly asking me for spankings instead.

Kids are smart enough to know that begging for a spanking is a lot like Briar Rabbit's classic escape trick. In the fable, Briar Rabbit had been caught by his enemy and knew that his only way of escaping was to plead, "Oh, please, Mr. Wolf, whatever you do, don't throw me in that briar patch."

Pearl 32

❖

STEALING

Of all the problems that surface with our kids, nothing affects our emotions quite as much as stealing. The right of property holds a high place in our moral hierarchy. We want our kids to respect what is theirs, and keep their hands off what isn't.

But children do steal things from time to time. Usually our kids' stealing cannot be cured by a direct frontal assault on the stealing itself. Instead, it has to be handled by understanding and reckoning with the underlying feelings that led to the act in the first place.

Fortunately, as with lying, early stealing—that is, between the ages of four and six—is almost always simply a childhood phase. If handled matter-of-factly, without too much anger, invariably most children quickly outgrow the stealing phase. An emotional response from us, however, usually makes matters worse, because kids get defensive and fight for control. Let's look at the two approaches in action.

Little Janice lifts an earring from her mom's jewelry box. Mom finds out and shrieks, "Janice, did you take this earring? . . . Don't just look at me, answer me. . . . I told you not to get in my jewelry box. This really makes me mad. You take it back right now. Don't you *ever* do that again!"

Without realizing it, this mom is teaching Janice to continue her stealing by vibrating so much emotion. The child will begin to feel insecure and start going our of her way to upset Mom. Stealing becomes kind of exciting for Janice — a lot of noise and no consequences.

A better way of handling the incident would have been for the mom to say, "Janice, honey, Mommy doesn't like it when you take her earring. Now, take it back to the box. Thank you. (Then, very excitedly) Oh, thank you for putting it back. That makes Mommy so happy. What a good girl."

By approaching it this way, Mom gives Janice good feelings for making sure the earring is put *into* the right place, not emotion because the earring was taken *from* the right place.

Chronic stealing, however, can be a different story. A parent-child control battle may be the cause, or the problem's roots may run deeper.

Stealing almost always occurs when a child is feeling empty or unloved. The feeling of emptiness can come on the child suddenly, or it can be long-term. The child may steal in much the same way as people bite their fingernails — by habit. Inside these kids are saying, "I'm not getting my fair share. I should have more."

With chronic stealing it is important for us to get at the underlying issue, whether it is a poor self-concept or the child's feeling of being "unfaired upon." Talking with our children (when the problem is not occurring), building their self-concept, and demonstrating our love for them will help tremendously.

Stealing is a multifaceted problem that usually cannot be dealt with directly. But children's feelings of loss, emptiness, or unfairness can be addressed with understanding, touch, eye contact, hugs, and the use of sensible, non-angry consequences.

Pearl 33

❖

SWEARING AND
BAD LANGUAGE

It hits us like an ice-water jacuzzi. That innocent little foundling we once dandled on our knees and whose vocabulary consisted exclusively of coos and goo-goos tramps through the door one day spewing forth a string of expletives that would make a dock worker blush.

Sometimes our kids are mimicking their school mates. Other times they seem to use obscenities merely to watch our neck hairs stand straight out. Whatever the reason, our children's bad language can be a troubling thing for us.

But in many cases it is a mere rite of passage, a phase kids go through on their journey to maturity. They hear older kids swearing, and wanting to be big like them, they develop a vocabulary more in tune with that used under an NBA backboard than in a Christian home.

We could respond with a diatribe of indignation: "You're not going to talk like that in this household! How many times have we told you to clean up that mouth?" Or, for that matter, we could take a cake of Lava to their teeth and gums. But then they'd only resolve all the more to exert their independence.

So our immediate response should be to move the problem out of earshot. Tell the child, without anger, "I'll be happy to talk with you when you can speak civilly to me and use clean and mature language." When both we and our child have calmed down, we should talk about the problem itself. One approach is to address the child's sense of worth: "Leon, I think a lot of people who use that sort of language are people who don't feel all that good about themselves."

Or we may want to take an intellectual tack: "Some people who use that sort of language have a very limited vocabulary, Leon. They don't know many words, so they pull out those boring old swear words and use them. Nobody has to look them up in the dictionary. They're really easy words. That's probably why some people use them, Leon."

Then we should drop the issue. The language our children use will, in the long run, be the language they want to use. White-hot anger on our part will only delay their realization that immature people resort to such language.

Pearl 34

❖

TEACHER AND
SCHOOL PROBLEMS

Generally, our role in our children's school life—in their marks and behavior—is concentrated on encouragement and good modeling. We leave the discipline to the teachers and administrators: We let our children handle their own school problems. But sometimes we may have to step in and approach a child's teacher. This is a difficult thing, for it often calls to mind all the feelings of intimidation we may have experienced with our own teachers.

When approaching a child's teacher, the attitude we should have is one of collecting information and thinking about it, rather than storming into the teacher's room and offering solutions. We can make three common mistakes.

Mistake one: We tell the teacher what to do. When we say, "I want my kid out of that classroom," what we are really telling the teacher is, "You aren't smart enough to figure out what to do, so I've got to help you."

Mistake two: We go into the school with threats. Saying, "If I don't get my way, I'm going to go to the principal" creates even more problems than we had when we came in.

Mistake three: We muster an army of like-minded parents to assault the teacher en masse. Any victory in this sort of confrontation will be short lived, for the teacher will fight for his or her life. A variation of this tactic is saying, "I'm not the only person who's upset with this. A lot of others are too. But I'm the only one with the nerve to come talk to you."

All of these tactics are serious mistakes. We may have walked into the school with a problem. But when we leave, we'll have a problem and an enemy. People in general, and teachers too, who are put on the defensive are less inclined to come up with thoughtful solutions to problems.

Parents who get the best results with teachers are ones who use the magic word *describe*. It's magic because when we use it we aren't telling the teacher anything. We're *describing* something: "I'd like to describe something that's happening, and then give you my interpretation of it." When we've had our say, we can then use more magic words: "I'd like to get your thoughts on that." By saying this, we are telling the teacher we have confidence that he or she can think for himself or herself.

Another approach is to say, "What kind of options are available to solve a problem like this," then sit back and allow the teacher to think awhile. Remember, as well as we think we know our children, we may not know how they react in a school environment. Children frequently are a lot different at school than at home. A child who is easy to work with on a one-on-one basis may be frustrated and unruly when given one-twenty-fifth of that attention. So, the teacher's reading of the situation is very helpful.

If we get no satisfaction with the teacher and want to kick the problem up the ladder, we should say, "Would you mind going with me to see if the principal has any thoughts on this?" That's a whole lot better than saying, "If I don't get my way, I'm going to the principal."

Our chief mission in approaching a teacher is to discuss our child's problem and see if a solution can be reached — to talk as well as listen, to suggest as well as take suggestions. Communication and respect for others are much more effective than commands and threats.

Pearl 35

---❖---

TEETH BRUSHING

Kids, like the rest of us, love second chances. Those awful mistakes they make aren't nearly so haunting when they know there's another chance if they blow the first one.

One great opportunity for our children to have a second chance looks right at us every time they flash us their big, happy grins. In fact, there are twenty second chances staring at us—their baby teeth. Children are given a whole mouthful to practice their brushing techniques on, and when they've done that for eleven or twelve years, they're given a brand-new set.

Getting kids to appreciate that opportunity can be a hassle, though. They grab their brush and tube after every meal with about the same relish as we grab our calculator and tax forms every April. One little swipe across the pearly whites with the bristles and they're ready to get on with living.

We can allow our kids to get in on the ground floor of conscientious dental hygiene and take the hassle out of the process all at the same time. But we have to be good models. Letting them see us brushing our teeth is effective, as is talking out loud to ourselves: "I just finished eating, and I think I'd better go protect my teeth with a little brushing."

Talking to our spouse is even more effective. One dad ended every meal by saying to his wife, "I sure can't go through the rest of the day with all that sugar on my teeth and in my mouth. I'd better go take care of it so I won't have cavities." He then trotted to the bathroom for a thorough brushing, and when he returned he talked to his wife again: "I'm sure glad I did that. It only took a couple of minutes to get the job done, and I feel a whole lot better." Kids can thus model what we say as well as how we feel after we've done it.

None of these kinds of comments can be too transparent for our eavesdropping children. They feel the excitement of overhearing something they think they shouldn't be hearing, and they're much more likely to try it for themselves than if we get in their faces about it.

As the "thrill" of brushing wears off, however, we may feel it necessary to get results by linking our kids' dental hygiene with things they want to do. Here, thinking words are the way to go: "You're welcome to go out to play as soon as your teeth are brushed," or "Feel free to watch television as soon as you brush your teeth."

One mom, before passing out cookies, prefaced the distribution with these words: "I pass out things with sugar in them to the people in this family who protect their teeth with brushing." Then she read roll call: "Noelle's been brushing her teeth, and Jill's been brushing hers, and Claudia . . . well, Claudia, we'd better hold off on cookies until I don't have to worry so much about your teeth anymore."

Claudia was a regular at the sink from that day on.

Pearl 36

❖

TELEPHONE INTERRUPTIONS

Young children just don't understand telephone eti-
quette. Why, they are even capable of choosing the exact
time when we are on the phone to ask us a question, hit us
with a request, or otherwise seek our attention. Although
much of the technology has changed, you still can't talk
to two different people about two different things at the
same time.

What usually happens is that the person on the other
end of the line hears something like this: "Yes, Mr. Bosseroo,
the Castleman report specifically stated . . . Angela! Quit
pulling on my pants! Sorry about that, sir, but the numbers
for the second quarter are in an obvious up . . . Angela!
Not now!" And Mr. Bosseroo — or whoever — thinks, "Why
doesn't this guy get control of his kid?"

The fact is, we are not chained to that telephone. We *can*
put it down. When we deal with the problem of interrupting
children in a rational way, it permits our callers to abandon
the notion that our domestic life resembles the floor of the
Chicago grain market. If we handle our insistent children in
a business-like way — "Mr. Bosseroo, it looks like something
has come up. Can you hang on for a second?" — our caller
will not think less of us. Then get down on the child's level

and briefly address him or her: "Angela, honey, you need to run up to your room for five minutes. When five minutes are up, I want to see you down here again, but with your mouth closed if I'm still on the telephone."

If Angela refuses, then we must deal with the problem more extensively. Saying to our caller, "Can I call you right back?" will give us that opportunity. Callers usually accept this technique. They can see that we are taking control of our children and not allowing them to control us. Plus, it's a lot more pleasant for them not having a human air-raid siren howling in the background.

Then, sometime when the phone is not ringing (Is there such a time?), we can pull our child onto our lap and hash it out:

DAD: "Angela, honey, I notice that whenever I'm talking on the phone you want to talk to me at the
same time. Do you have any thoughts on that?"
ANGELA: "I wanted to show you Cinderella and the
wicked sisters. See?"
DAD: "Yes, Angela. Let me look at it for a minute. . . .
That's very pretty coloring. But I can only do
one thing at a time, dear. When I'm talking on
the phone, I can look at your Cinderella and the
wicked sisters only a little. But when I'm not on
the phone, I can look at them a lot."
ANGELA: "But I wanted you to look at them when
you were on the phone!"
DAD: "Well, I'm thinking that I could look at them a
lot better when I'm not talking on the telephone.
I really would like to look at them a lot, but I
can't then because I have to talk to the person on
the telephone. If you can show me your coloring
when I can look a little or when I can look a lot,
which do you think would be better?"
ANGELA: "When you can look at them a lot."

DAD: "Right. And when would that be?"
ANGELA: "When you're not talking on the phone."

This technique is also effective with kids who interrupt discussions between parents, or between a parent and another adult.

The message given to the child is that their interruptions are a problem, and we don't like it. When it happens, the child must go somewhere else and think about it.

Pearl 37

❖

TELEVISION WATCHING

Every new media-use study brings on another bout of parental anxiety. The headlines are alarming: "Average child watches five hours of television a day, study says," or "Experts claim television dominant influence in average American kids' lives." We read the reports, cast a wary eye toward the family room where our kids are imitating potted plants in front of the tube, and we shake our heads in dismay. "Those kids," we say, "watch too much television!"

Television watching—What programs? How much time? When? Why?—is the source of many parent-child tiffs. Maybe as much blood has been shed over kids watching television as has been portrayed on the screen itself. We are forever devising strategies to curtail our kids' television habits.

But with television watching, as with many other issues, our modeling is the key. It's pretty unreasonable for major league couch potatoes, who hit the "on" button at the opening theme of "Good Morning America" and the "off" button after the last sick joke on "Late Night with David Letterman," to come down hard on their children's television habits.

That we must be aware of our own viewing habits is fairly obvious. But there's more. If we are more interesting to our children then the stuff that comes over the tube, then they will prefer being with us. A simple "Let's go make that birdhouse now, what do you say, Rob?" or, "Okay, Linda, are you ready to take on your mom at Chinese Checkers?" or, "Come on out in the driveway, Carl, and Dad will show you the fine points of his world-famous sky hook" often will pry our kids away from the box. Most kids would much rather do something else, as long as it's with someone they love.

To influence our kids' television habits, we must emphasize the alternatives, playing up the good things about friends, family, hobbies, sports, and so on. Consider this discussion between a dad and a television-watching son:

> DAD: "I've noticed that you're watching a lot of television lately, Tad. You like it, don't you?"
>
> TAD: "Yeah, I like it a lot."
>
> DAD: "The good thing about TV is that you can learn from it. You can find out what's happening in the world, it helps your vocabulary, and you can learn about grown-ups. But one thing I'm wondering about is how much do you think you learn about being a good friend on TV? Are you a good friend to our TV set?"
>
> TAD: "I don't know what you mean."
>
> DAD: "Right. Because the television doesn't listen much to you, does it? It just talks at you. It doesn't care about what you say, right?"
>
> TAD: "Uh, right."
>
> DAD: "So, one thing about a TV set is it doesn't help you to be a good friend of anybody else. Does it ever pay attention to what you say?"
>
> TAD: "No."
>
> DAD: "What I think about TV, Tad, is that it really doesn't care what you think. That's the problem with the TV. Whereas your friends and I listen

to you. I think if you watch a lot of television
you can be smart about many things. But I don't
know if you'll ever be able to prove it because
you don't learn how to talk by watching TV. You
might be happier in the long run if you watch
less. But whose decision is it?"

TAD: "Mine."

DAD: "Yes, it really is. Hey, let me feel your brain. It
doesn't feel too soft—yet!"

It's best not to set ourselves up for a control battle over
television watching with commands and threats. Harping at
our kids constantly, or imposing severe cuts in their viewing
habits, often leads to rebellion.

What we can do, however, is influence our kids. A gen-
erous dose of humor does wonders. Pushing on their heads
as they watch television and declaring, "Well, it's not too
soft yet," sends them the message that too much television
will turn their brains to oat bran.

I (Foster) once reminisced, for the benefit of my son
Jerry, about a brain operation I had performed as a neuro-
surgeon: "I remember my last neurosurgery case. This guy
came in who was a little spacey. We couldn't figure out
what was wrong with him; the X-rays didn't show much.
So we put him on the table and anesthetized him, then did
some burr holes in his head. Guess what happened? His
brains flowed out the holes like thin cottage cheese. We
couldn't understand it. Then we checked his file again, and
there it was, clear as day. This guy had watched TV four
hours a day for the past six weeks."

Jerry's eyes popped out like a pirate's telescope because
he had been watching four hours of television a day for the
past *six years!*

In the long run, our kids will decide not to watch too
much television because *they* have found other things to do
or believe it's not good for them.

Pearl 38

❖

TEMPER TANTRUMS

There's usually a little warning—that's the good news. First we see the big ear-to-ear frown. Next the flushing of the face. Then the balled up little fists. Sometimes the little lips twitch spasmodically as a sort of warmup exercise. All of these preliminaries give us a few seconds to sprint for the earmuffs before the little mouth opens wide and fills the room with a scream that would run shivers up and down Stephen King's spine.

The temper tantrum. Every child has his or her own style. Some plop their fannies down on the floor in preparation, others latch onto our legs as if they were tree trunks in a windstorm, and others fall back on tradition—the pounding-fists-on-the-floor routine. It actually could be sort of humorous—if it were someone else's kid, and we had suitable ear protection in place.

The bad news is that temper tantrums happen regardless of what we do. At one time or another, every kid throws one. Unfortunately, many parents approach these tantrums with fear and loathing. They try to do everything humanly possible to prevent them, even to the point of avoiding saying no to their tyke for fear that the little fellow will explode like Mount Saint Helens.

Two things to remember about tantrums: One, *any kid worth keeping will probably throw a fit from time to time.* Only kids whose spirits have been broken don't fight to get their way. Two, *kids will throw tantrums only as long as they work.* Odd, isn't it, that kids never seem to scream and pound the floor when they're alone in their room? The show goes on when they have a guaranteed audience.

Wise parents simply let tantrums happen. There's nothing we can do to stop them anyway. What we can do, however, is to change the location. We don't change *that* it is happening, we change *where.*

"I give that tantrum a 7.5," one parent told his howling Hannah. "It's not world-class, but it's pretty good for a local girl. Now, where would you like to have that tantrum so it won't disturb my ears?"

"Wa-a-a-a-a!" Hannah screams, pounding her fists on the floor and kicking at the air.

"It's up to an 8.2 now. Would you like to have it in the basement, or in your room?"

"Ho-o-o-w-l-l-l!" Hannah shrieks from by the refrigerator, on which she is banging her head to emphasize her point.

"Oh, this is definitely a basement tantrum, Hannah. Hang on, I'll open the door. By the way, do you want the light on or off?"

You get the idea. Give a few choices and get them downwind of you. Nothing in the parenting almanac says we have to put up with abuse like that, so we remove the children from our presence. We allow them to return when the hurricane dies down to a light drizzle.

Some parents combat tantrums with the "Giant Step Technique," as in taking a giant step over the wailing child while heading for the door as quickly as possible, trying to leave the house before he or she can say, "Wait for me." At least "Wait for me" is not a tantrum. (But note well: That's a step *over* the child, not *on* him or her.)

The last thing we want to do is to lose our composure, screaming back at our kids or saying, "You just keep on screaming, and I'll give you something to really scream about!" Handling temper tantrums requires parents with soft voices who don't even try to reason with their misbehaving child. The message we want to send is, "That behavior is okay for now, as long as I don't have to see or hear it."

Some parents are concerned about children hurting themselves while throwing tantrums. These parents should childproof the room, removing all dangerous or valuable objects. However, extreme violence rarely will occur if the audience is removed. If the children do hurt themselves, however, drive the lesson home with sadness over their injury when the tantrum is over. (In families where this is a severe problem, professional counseling may be advised.)

Pearl 39

❖

TOILET TRAINING

Brace yourselves for this one, folks: Toilet training is fun!
"What?" you shriek. "Tell me about it. All that hassle just
getting kids onto the potty chair. Then when we get them
there, you'd think they'd go, right? Think again. They sit
there for a few seconds, then stand right up, declare, 'All
done!' and hie off to the corner of the living room and do
their dirty work *there*. Then there's all that doo-doo to clean
up. Fun? It's about as much fun as toxic waste!"

Okay, okay, we lied. What we meant to say was, "Toilet
training *can be* fun—for us and for our kids." But first,
the facts:

◆ Some children are naturally easy to toilet train and
  really train themselves.
◆ Some children are very difficult to train.
◆ Children differ developmentally. Some are ready at
  age two, while others may not be ready until four-
  and-a-half.
◆ It is essential to keep the feelings around toilet
  training fun, exciting—even gleeful.
◆ It is all too easy for a vicious cycle of negativism
  to swirl up around toilet training because we have

a vested interest in their potty habits. We really *do* want them to go into the pot. For the first time in their lives, we really want them to do something for *us*.

Keeping these facts in mind, we can approach the stool, so to speak, not like it's some kind of torture we all must submit to several times a day, but with an enthusiastic and happy attitude. If *we* consider it a chore, our kids will follow suit.

Bear in mind, there is an anatomical difference between boys and girls. What works for one, won't work for the other. Annie draws pictures for her little daughter Heather while they talk:

> ANNIE: "Look, here's the kitty going potty in the hole that she digs. Look how happy the kitten is!"
> HEATHER: "Is she happy?"
> ANNIE: "Oh, she's so happy she's putting it there. All animals are different. Now, here's a doggie. He likes to go on a tree. Boy, is he happy. You know what? I want to make myself happy, so I'm going to go into the bathroom right now and put my pee-pee in the potty. I feel so good when I do that!"
> HEATHER: "Can I do it too?"
> ANNIE: "Oh, that would be wonderful, but not until I get to do it first."

With boys we can get right down to a little first-person modeling action. Larry plays "Sink the Bismarck" with his little son Alex:

> LARRY: "I take this toilet paper and I wad it up, Alex, and I throw it in there and you know what that is?"
> ALEX: "No."

LARRY: "That's a PT boat. And here's another one, a
  battleship. Can you guess what I'm going to do,
  Alex?"
ALEX: "No."
LARRY: "I'm going to sink them all. Watch!"
ALEX: "Can I do that, too?"
LARRY: "If you're a good shot. But you have to be
  quick, because they sink by themselves pretty
  fast."

Some parents tape two suckers to the bathroom door
for post-duty enjoyment, not as a bribe, but because kids
and parents feel so good when they're done that they feel
they both deserve them.

One tactic to avoid, however, is the "you sit there until
you go" routine. It can cause a lot of hard feelings and is
usually ineffective.

Pearl 40

❖

VALUES: PASSING THEM ON TO YOUR KIDS

Every day it seems there's another story of the decline in values in our youth in the United States. Drugs are a scourge on the land, available even in remote rural schools. Teenage pregnancy is skyrocketing. In many schools, teachers are more police officers than they are instructors. A troubling materialism rears its ugly head even among elementary school students. In our society, proper moral values seem to be taking a pretty good licking.

As parents, this disturbing trend brings the cold sweat of responsibility to our furrowed brows. "I want my children to have responsible moral values," we say. "But how do I teach them those values?"

A great wave of change has swept over our society in the past forty years. The "human rights" revolution has spread even to our children. Parents cannot make their kids think like they do simply by telling them "You'll do it or else." Demands and threats may yield short-term results, but they don't mold our kids' minds. They don't persuade them that we're right.

In a real sense, parenting *is* the transmitting of our values to our kids. We want our kids to be honest; we want them to respect others; we want them to know the value of hard work; we want a moral and ethical lifestyle to be as important to them as it is to us.

There's bad news and good news in this question of transmitting values, however. The bad news is that we can't stroll down the wide and easy road of lecturing our kids on the topic. It might have worked for our parents, but the odds for success have radically tipped the other way. The good news, though, is that it *is* still possible to pass on our values to our kids. But it's going to take some effort—and thought.

Values are passed on to children in two ways: by what our kids *see*, and by what they *experience in relating to us*. When our kids see us being honest, they learn about honesty. When we talk to our kids with love and respect, they learn to talk that way to others.

We can accelerate our modeling effectiveness by engaging in "eavesdrop value setting." That means that Mom and Dad talk to each other about their values, but within earshot of the kids. If we want our children to learn about honesty, for example, we allow them to overhear us reporting on our genuine acts of honesty. "You know, sweetie," we might say to our spouse, "something interesting happened to me today. At the store I gave the clerk a five-dollar bill for a can of pop and she gave me $14.50 in change. A Hamilton must have got stuck in with her Washingtons. So, I gave her back the ten. I could have said nothing and been $10 richer, but I feel so much better being honest—doing what's right."

Or, if our peers relate some off-color and demeaning stories at work, we may say to our spouse, when our kids can overhear us, "The guys at the office were telling dirty stories today in the lunchroom, but I excused myself and ate lunch at my desk. It always bothers me to hear stories like that, and I feel bad if I stick around just so the others think I'm part of the gang. I feel much better for thinking for myself and walking away."

Kids soak up what they hear when we speak to others.

It's great when what they soak up is good. But be advised, they're sponges for the bad, too.

Our improper words and actions hit them with the same force. If we have nothing but ridicule for our bosses and coworkers, our kids learn that ridicule and sarcasm are an acceptable way to talk. If we cheat at board games or when we play sports with our young children, then we shouldn't wring our hands and cry, "Why?" when they get nailed for cheating at school. If our idea of a good time is a La-Z-Boy recliner, a six-pack of brew, and an NFL doubleheader, our kids will get the message that that's the way grownups have fun. All of our wise words to the contrary won't blunt that point.

The other way we influence our kids' values is in the way we treat them. A corollary to the Golden Rule applies here: Kids will do to others as their parents do to them. Treating our kids with respect teaches them to go and do likewise. Being fair with our kids makes them want to be fair to their friends and teachers.

Kids have minds of their own. They want to exert their independence and do their own thinking. They shuck off the things that are forced onto them and embrace the things they want to believe. If we want to pass our values down to them, we must present those values in a way that our kids can accept: in our actions and words. Kids' values come from what they see and hear — and also *over*hear. They don't accept what we try to drive into their heads with lecturing.

Pearl 41

❖

WHINING AND COMPLAINING

It's ten o'clock in the morning and Mikey wants a cookie. He knows he can't have one, but that has never stopped him from asking before, and it won't stop him now. "Mommy, I want a cookie," he whines, his little fist clutching the seam on his mom's jeans.

"Mikey, you know you can't have cookies between meals," Mom returns. "Now, run off and play."

"But, Mommy, I want one," Mikey continues.

"You can have one at lunchtime. Now, off you go."

"Mommy, but I don't want to wait. I want one now."

"Well, you can't have one."

"But, Mom-m-my. I want one now-w-w!"

Then it happens. Parents who tolerate whining from their kids eventually whine back. "Will you stop whin-n-ning?" Mom says. "I *hate* it when you whine like that!"

No wonder Mikey whines like a pro—he has a good teacher. The fact is, parents who spend a lot of time pleading with their children develop kids who are experts at pleading. Quite often, just to get rid of that long-playing singsongy record of complaint, we surrender and grudgingly fork over the cookie. The message the child gets is that whining works.

The secret to handling whiny behavior is similar to that of combatting disrespect. Our children must learn that they will get no results whatsoever until the tone of voice changes.

Some school teachers effectively fight whiny behavior with multiple-choice questions. Once I (Jim) heard a teacher say, "Do you suppose I'll be able to understand you better when you're whining or not whining? Why don't you go to your desk and think about that? Come back when you've decided."

We can do the same. Saying, "When your voice sounds like mine, I'll be glad to talk with you," addresses the real problem with whining: the child's tone of voice. Whether or not Mikey can have a cookie will be discussed later, after the syrupy, high-pitched pleading stops. But kids are nothing if not persistent. Sometimes saying, "I won't listen to you while you're whining," encourages them and provides the emotional feedback they want. By saying it we may actually be responding to their whining. What then?

If we think we aren't getting results by asking them to leave, or if we find ourselves drawn into a discussion, then we can win the battle by ignoring the whining altogether. It is best, however, to explain this method before employing it. Sit the child down when emotions are calm and say, "Mikey, if Mom and I ever act like we don't hear you, it's not because we don't hear you. We do hear you. It's just that we don't want to hear you unless you talk a certain way. That's why we won't answer your question. But when you can talk nicely, in the same tone of voice we talk in, then you'll get an answer."

Eventually, kids will realize that we'll only listen when they're speaking civilly.

INDEX

225

LOVE AND LOGIC SEMINARS

Foster Cline, M.D., and Jim Fay present "Love and Logic" seminars for both parents and educators in many cities each year. For more information on their cassette tapes, seminars, or other helpful materials, contact:

Cline/Fay Institute, Inc.
Fay Professional Building, Suite 102
2207 Jackson Street
Golden, CO 80401
1-800-338-4065